Pot Bla

Compiled by Re

BRITISH BROADCASTING CORPORATION

Published by the British Broadcasting Corporation,
35 Marylebone High Street, London W1M 4AA
ISBN 0 563 20293 9
First published 1975
New revised edition 1984
© The British Broadcasting Corporation 1984
The Rules of Snooker © The Billiards
and Snooker Control Council.

Diagrams by Designline

Filmset by August Filmsetting, Haydock, St Helens
Printed in England by Hazell, Watson and Viney Ltd,
Aylesbury

The help of the following is gratefully acknowledged:
The Billiards and Snooker Control Council;
Powerglide Cues Ltd; Snooker Promotions Ltd;
Clive Everton, editor of *Snooker Scene*; Ted Lowe;
E.A. Clare & Son, Liverpool; Thomas Padmore &
Sons Ltd; The Composition Billiards Ball Supply Co.
Ltd.
The cartoon on page 14 is reproduced by kind
permission of the *Daily Mail*. Other pictures
are reproduced as follows: pages 27, 43, 47, 53, 57,
59, 63, 65, 69, 72, 77, 83, 89, 96, 107, 113, 117,
121, 123, 128, 131, 136, 141, 151, 153, 154, 156,
158, 162, 170 *bottom left* David Muscroft; 109, 160
All-Sport (Adrian Murrell): 170 *top & bottom right,*
171 Cue World; all other pictures are BBC copyright.

Cover picture taken at West Ealing Snooker Club by
Steve Benbow/Network.

Contents

Foreword

When *Pot Black* began in 1969 professional snooker was in the 'doldrums'. Joe Davis had long retired from competitive play and Steve Davis was a twelve-year-old schoolboy.

No one – either in the BBC or among the eight players who appeared in the first series – could possibly have foreseen the programme's eventual success and corresponding influence upon the game itself. I have enjoyed the privilege of working on every series from 1969 to 1983 together with the added pleasure of producing its offspring – *Junior Pot Black*.

This particular amateur competition has 'discovered' such talented young players – now professionals – as Neal Foulds, Dean Reynolds, John Parrott and, recently, Dene O'Kane.

Pot Black now celebrates its seventeenth year and in wishing the programme continued success, I also thank all those who have supported the series throughout this time and especially our millions of faithful and enthusiastic viewers.

Reg Perrin

Pot Black: The Game
by Reg Perrin

When Steve Davis won the 1984 World Professional Snooker Championship his winner's cheque for £44,000 was the highest individual prize in the history of the game. The first World Championship had been instituted and won in 1927 by the late Joe Davis, who had persuaded the governing body of the day, the Billiards Association and Control Council, to approve such a competition, but their agreement stipulated that he should provide the trophy himself out of the attendance and entrance money. The silver cup that Steve lifted aloft in triumph in May 1984 was bought by Joe Davis in 1927 for £6.10s.0d!

Joe had begun his long and successful career as a billiards player but eventually realised that a greater potential public and commercial interest lay in the hardly considered game of snooker. Snooker had been born, if not out of contempt, certainly out of familiarity. Its great-grandfather, the game of billiards, had been played in various forms for over three hundred years, but billiards as we know it, using only three balls, had become for many repetitive and monotonous. A good player was able to score endless cannons by keeping the three balls closely bunched together. Games became never-ending with astronomical scores – the record was 499,315 (unfinished!) set up by Tom Reece in 1907 and took five weeks to achieve. Breaks of over 2000 are common and billiards, as a spectator sport, has gradually gone into a decline.

There are anachronistic references to billiards in Shakespeare's *Antony and Cleopatra* (Act 2 scene 5), but its origins are even earlier. It was developed over a considerable period of time via a game called 'paille maille', played in France in the fifteenth century. This was a form of croquet played with wooden balls and clubs. The popularity of the sport brought it to England during the Stuart period, and one of its venues in London gave rise to the name of the famous Pall Mall. The game was then 'miniaturised', becoming an indoor pastime, and was played on a special table using a 'mace' – the forerunner of today's cue. The mace, resembling a thin, blunt-ended hockey-stick, was used to push the balls through various hoops on the table – at this time there were no 'pockets'. (Even today the billiard tables in Europe are pocket-less, and the French and Belgians play a game called 'carambolage' where points are scored by cannons and making extensive use of the side cushions.)

In 1674 the *Complete Gamester* quoted billiards as being 'a most gentile, cleanly and ingenious game', but for over a century the game progressed only slowly until, in the 1820s, a London cabinet-maker, John Thurston, became intrigued with the game and gave it a new lease of life by completely revolutionising the design of the table. He replaced the wooden bed with slate, the stuffed cushions with indiarubber and the maces with thin, pointed cues. A French army officer, Captain Mingaud, invented a leather tip for the cue which, when applied with chalk, gave a higher degree of control on the cue-ball than had hitherto been possible, thus introducing the use of side, screw, stun, etc.

By 1852 'named' players were beginning to emerge. One of them, Edwin Kentfield, had in 1833 written his *Treatise on Billiards*, now a much sought-after collector's item. Tables became in demand overseas, especially where British troops were stationed. Which is where the story of snooker really begins! The *Radio Times* Television Supplement for 9 April 1937 stated: 'The origin of snooker is obscure, but the introduction of the game is attributed to Captain Snooker who was an officer in the Bengal Lancers in India.'

As far as is known today, 'Captain Snooker' never existed. There is now another and well-authenticated account of the game's origin. In the latter half of the nineteenth century variations on the theme of billiards included 'Pyramids', 'Pool' and 'Black Pool', where vari-ous coloured balls had been added to the traditional two whites and a red. In Jubbulpore, India, in 1875, a group of Army officers were playing Black Pool on the mess billiards table when a young subaltern, Sir Neville Cham-berlain, suggested the addition of other coloured balls with different scoring values. During the progress of this new game one of Sir Neville's opponents failed to pot a ball, leaving Sir Neville with an unplayable shot. 'Gad sir,

6

you're a regular snooker!' was the angry outburst from Sir Neville. (A snooker was the nickname for a first-year cadet at Woolwich Military Academy and obviously held in very low regard.) However, regaining his composure, Sir Neville admitted that they were all 'snookers' at the game, and thus it was christened.

Before long, rumours of this new game of 'snooker' reached England and a well-known professional billiards player, John Roberts, travelled to India to learn about the game at first hand. He was introduced to Sir Neville Chamberlain in Calcutta by the Maharajah of Cooch Behar, the new rules were explained to him, and Roberts returned to England to demonstrate snooker to his colleagues. In 1891 John Dowland, another professional player, drew up the first set of recognised rules and the game became established in the UK. Colonel Sir Neville Chamberlain died on 28 May 1944 aged eighty-eight. His memories of having 'invented' snooker were related to the novelist Sir Compton Mackenzie and published in the *Billiard Player* in its April 1939 issue.

Although an Amateur Snooker Championship was instituted in 1916 and a few Regional Professional Championships had been played in the early 1920s, it was Joe Davis who was responsible both for the development of snooker as a spectator sport and for devising the techniques of play which are now taken for granted by today's professionals. Having established the first World Snooker Championship he won the event every year until 1946. It is somewhat surprising, therefore, that the first demonstration of snooker on BBC Television was given, in April 1937, not by Joe but by two of his contemporaries, Willie Smith and Horace Lindrum. Joe's début from the studios at Alexandra Palace was on 3 May 1937 when he and Tom Newman gave a ten-minute demonstration of billiards.

After Joe retired, undefeated, from World Championship play in 1947, he continued to play in lesser tournaments and exhibition matches, and in the early 1960s competed in several 'challenge' games on BBC TV's *Grandstand* (I had the pleasure of directing many of them). The first 147 maximum break to be eventually ratified as a world record was, once again, made by the great Joe at the Leicester Square Hall on 22 January 1955. He was now fifty-three and had been playing for thirty-five years, with a staggering total of 574 century breaks to his credit. He was awarded the OBE in 1963 for his services to charity and, when he finally retired from the game in 1964, he vowed never to play again – not even in the privacy of his own billiards room. Nevertheless he maintained an active interest in the game in all its aspects as President of the Players' Association.

Pot Black, one of the early colour programmes on BBC2, was first seen on 23 July 1969. From 1970 onwards Joe, having given the programme his approval, became an annual guest and presented the trophy to the *Pot Black* champions. In 1971 – despite his vow – he was even persuaded to take his cue from its dusty case and play some trick-shots! In 1976 the programme had the privilege of presenting Joe with the *Pot Black* Personality Award – a miniature trophy.

The eight players who competed in the first two *Pot Black* series in 1969–70 were Rex Williams, Ray Reardon, John Pulman, Jack Rea, Gary Owen, the late Kingsley Kennerley, John Spencer and Joe's 'younger' brother Fred. Eighteen other leading professionals have appeared in the series up to 1984 – David Taylor, Eddie Charlton, Alex Higgins, Graham Miles, Cliff Thorburn, Dennis Taylor, Willie Thorne, Perrie Mans, Doug Mountjoy, Jim Wych, Kirk Stevens, Terry Griffiths, Steve Davis, Tony Knowles, Jimmy White, Tony Meo, Silvino Francisco and Mark Wildman.

Today the snooker industry is thriving both as a sport, where hundreds of youngsters take up the game each year, and as a commercial enterprise. The name of *Pot Black* has been used to christen snooker tables, cues, badges, snooker clubs, a magazine and, aptly enough, to advertise a certain well-known brand of Irish stout! Snooker writers and the press have been unanimous in their verdict that television, and *Pot Black* in particular, has played a paramount role in dispelling the game's 'seedy' image of the past, creating instead a colourful shop-window for a game 'invented' by a group of Indian Army officers over a hundred years ago.

The table

An important ingredient in the *Pot Black* series is the table. Many viewers probably never think twice about it or, if they do, assume that the Snooker Table has not really altered in design or construction since the game was invented. But the Billiard Table, to give it its correct name, and its equipment have slowly evolved in construction and design over a very long period of time. (In Britain and the Commonwealth, there is now a tendency for players to call the tables 'Snooker Tables' and to purchase 'Snooker Cues', and even to ask for 'Snooker Chalk'.)

Whilst Britain plays the game of 'English billiards' and 'snooker', most European countries play 'carambolage' or 'Continental billiards' – the principal difference being that the Continental-style tables do not have any pockets and the game is entirely made up of a series of cannons, while the English table has pockets at each corner and at the centre of each long side. (In the United States a large number of different games, all of which we generally refer to as 'American pool', are played on tables which have pockets, but with a population of mixed European origin billiards follows the Continental style: tables without pockets.)

A full-sized billiard table is twelve foot long, six foot wide and about two foot ten inches high. The timbers most commonly used are mahogany, oak and walnut, and in the nineteenth century the bed of the table itself was also made of wood. In the second half of the nineteenth century tables manufactured in Liverpool had cast-iron underframes. These tables stood on six legs and one of them was in use in a staff canteen in Liverpool until a few years ago.

The actual 'bed' of the billiard table is now made of slate, although it was once made of iron. Such tables were to be found in Ireland at the beginning of this century, but obviously these 'iron beds' suffered from the damp atmosphere and would develop rust, thus staining the cloth. It was also very difficult to unscrew the nuts and bolts in order to move and reassemble a table. Experiments have recently been carried out with 'glass' beds, but there is still nothing better in sight than a slate bed. The advantages are that slate is easy to cut, to drill and to plane the surface; even in the course of wear, when small pieces may be chipped off the edges, it is reasonably easy to repair the damage using modern filler materials.

The first slate beds were introduced by John Thurston about 1834. The slates then were about one inch thick, but as time went on they became thicker and today a slate bed has to be two inches thick if it is going to be satisfactory. Each slab weighs between three and four hundredweight and requires four men to handle it. The total weight of a billiard table is therefore about one and three-quarter tons. So if you are toying with the idea of installing one in the lounge, make sure the floorboards are sound!

Table maintenance

Ensure that the table is brushed daily. This prevents dust and chalk-dust penetrating the cloth and forming uneven ridges on the slate. Brush the cushion cloths before the bed cloth. Always brush from baulk to spot end – along the nap of the cloth. Use a dust cover whenever the table is not in use, especially overnight.

After a period of six months or so the cloth should be removed so that dust and other particles can be cleaned off from the slate. At this time the cloth needs to be stretched, which will help prevent cue-damage. This will not only double the life of the cloth, but the balls will run faster and truer. When ironing, make sure that the iron is clean. Use a moderate heat – too hot an iron will discolour the cloth. As with brushing, ironing should be from the baulk to the top of the table and the iron should be lifted carefully at the end of the table to prevent damage to the cushions.

The cue

The original cue bore very little resemblance to the cue as it is today. The general shape was similar, as it was necessary to reach across the table in the same way as now. It had a normal cue-like shaft, but with a wooden head, two to three inches wide and not unlike a small rake without the spikes, the balls being pushed or manoeuvred around the table. The name given to the 'cue' was a 'mace'. Some mystery surrounds the evolvement of the modern-day cue, but it is generally thought that probably the first variation was to turn the mace shaft around and strike the ball with the thin end. Later a leather tip was added and finally the 'mace' head was discarded. Probably the only trace of the 'mace' in its modern counterpart is the flat on the butt end of the cue. During the Victorian period it was accepted that the cue could be turned around and placed on to the table, allowing the ball to be struck with the butt end. The ladies appear to have been the main culprits for this action, since it would have been unladylike to lean or stretch across the table.

The most important requirement for a first-class straight cue is high-quality timber, but in this modern age of mass production of all kinds of furniture for the home and industry this becomes progressively more difficult to obtain. The most popular timber for cues is sporting ash, coppice-grown and straight-grained. This sounds easy, but good-quality ash has to be tracked down and reserved. The importance of the specification has to be impressed on the timber mill, since constant attention must be paid to the drying or moisture content of the material. If it is dried too fast the material will bend, making the manufacture of the cue far more difficult. On the other hand, if the moisture content is too high, it is most difficult to control the humidity loss, probably the most important reason for cues warping. If you extract the remaining moisture from any cue, it will bend like a bow; even bright lights or at least the heat that the lights generate will all help to dry out your cue.

The next most popular wood is Canadian maple, a good, strong, sound timber with slightly less troublesome humidity factor, since the grain formation of maple is much closer, with less softwood between the grain (softwood acts like blotting paper and allows moisture to be added or extracted with ease). Maple is the most popular cue-wood in North America, where the stabilising of the moistute content is all-important in club rooms and houses that are constantly kept at temperatures in excess of 70°F. Needless to say, North America is probably the most difficult part of the world to keep cues in good condition.

Probably the most confusing point to a beginner is the choice of a cue with the ideal weight. From the manufacturer's point of view the ideal weight is probably about $16\frac{1}{2}$ to 17 ounces, as this means that very little extra weight has to be added into the butt of the cue. This can produce the cue of ideal balance, well forward. If the cue is supported on your index finger at approximately the points of the splice it should ideally tilt forward so that when cueing it will lie into the playing bridge. This does not of course mean that a cue with a balance well back cannot be played with effectively.

The main use of the ferrule (the brass collar at the top end of the cue) is to avoid the cue shortening too quickly through constant retipping and levelling of the ferrule over the years (it is surprising how quickly this can happen). It also adds strength to a piece of timber that is, after all, only 10–11 mm thick, and could obviously quite easily split, as the power used on contact with the cue-ball is quite considerable. Tips are a constant worry to most players and the more competent the player the more worry they become. No two tips have the same playing quality: some are soft and spongy – not an ideal tip; some are very hard, which can be nearly as bad. A good tip can make the screw shot as easy as ABC.

Cues can go sticky, impregnated with a mixture of natural oils and dirt, and far too common a remedy for this is the use of sandpaper. Many a good cue is ruined by sandpapering, which removes both the artificial and the natural sealing agent, and once again allows the timber to dry out too quickly. The correct method is simple: a slightly dampened cloth rubbed up and down the shaft to remove any dirt and then a brisk rub with a clean dry cloth. This dries the cue thoroughly and produces a silky sheen that is a delight to handle.

The balls

The original billiard ball was made of ivory, and in the nineteenth century thousands of elephants were slaughtered to provide them. By 1890 nearly 15,000 cwt of ivory a year were passing through the Port of London and around 12,000 elephants a year were being killed for their tusks. On average, only four balls could be made from each tusk, and, as the density of the tusk varied considerably, only one or two of the four could be classed as top quality. To obtain a good set of billiard balls, therefore, might need seven or eight tusks.

An increasing demand for billiard balls and the growing scarcity of ivory led to experimentation with various substitutes. Peter Kinnear, a Scot who had emigrated to the United States in the 1860s and settled in Albany, about 150 miles from New York City, set to work to discover a substitute that would be cheaper and better than ivory. The problem was to find a suitable filler, and finally a friend called Hyatt, a chemist who subsequently invented the ball-bearing, discovered a perfect solution in the chemical cellulose nitrate, now known as celluloid.

In 1868 the Albany Billiard Ball Company was formed and produced the Hyatt ball, which was sold towards the end of the century in England by the Bonzoline Manufacturing Co. Ltd under the name of 'Bonzoline'. In 1900 George Birt left the Albany Company and came to England, where with Percy Warnford-Davis he started to produce the crystalate ball, a composition ball with a cellulose nitrate base, very similar to the Hyatt ball. In 1909 the Endolithic Company Ltd (who were marketing the crystalate ball) brought over from Australia the sensational young player George Gray, who made a series of the largest breaks ever made on a billiard table and established the reputation of the crystalate ball, after which it was adopted as the standard ball for all matches by the Billiards Association and Control Club.

Meanwhile a chemical firm in Germany was experimenting with the production of an entirely different type of ball with a phenol and formaldehyde base, the cast resin ball. It was rather lighter but had beautiful bright colours and a very attractive translucent appearance. The experiments were carried out by a brilliant German chemist, Dr Koebner, who in 1937 fled to London as a refugee. From then until his death twelve years later, he worked for the Billiard Ball Company, where a ball similar to the German product was perfected and marketed under the name 'vitalite'.

The cellulose nitrate type of ball was moulded from powder under great pressure and the resulting block of plastic material was turned and polished in a similar way to the old ivory ball, but the new cast resin ball was made by a much more modern and sophisticated process. The raw materials were mixed under heat in large stills until they produced a syrupy substance. This syrup was poured into glass flasks and then underwent a number of baking treatments lasting several days. Once again a hard block of plastic material was produced and had to be finished into a perfect sphere by means of a series of grinding and polishing operations on highly specialised machinery. The beautiful bright colours are obtained by adding aniline dyes during distillation.

However, for some years past it had been realised that the cellulose nitrate ball was becoming out of date as the raw materials became more difficult to obtain, and that the

13

time had come to produce something better and more modern. After intensive experimentation, therefore, 'Super Crystalate' was put on the market in 1972. This ball has specially bright and attractive colours, is very hard and durable and its specific density is very similar to crystalate, or rather heavier than vitalite. It has been an instant success and has been adopted by the Billiards Association and is now exclusively used by the leading professionals. It is the ball used in *Pot Black*, where millions can see how well the balls respond to the players' skill.

'That's the sign of a great player—always chalks his cue before beating his opponent over the head with it.'

Pot Black: The Programme

A 'broadcasting phenomenon' was how one distinguished critic described *Pot Black*. The dictionary records a phenomenon as being an extraordinary happening; yet, in 1969, when the programme first appeared on BBC2, mainly as an experiment to extend the potential of colour programmes, it certainly never occurred to anyone associated with it that it would quickly establish itself as a huge television success.

Reg Perrin, the producer from 1971 to 1983, recalls: 'We had a few mild reservations at the beginning. How would people react to the innovation of one-frame snooker? And would we ever be able to tempt an audience inside the studio to watch it?' Those mild reservations have long since evaporated, and without wishing to invite any charges of immodesty on our part, *Pot Black* is now internationally acclaimed as the biggest shop-window ever in professional snooker.

We have often tried to analyse why this is so, and perhaps the simple explanation is that snooker is tailor-made for television. It is the one sport in which television illustrates perfectly the expertise of the top professional's technique in close-up. In cricket coverage, for example, you never see how a player uses his wrist in his bowling action or in his batting. But in snooker viewers can see the player's bridge hand and how he holds the cue. There is no gimmickry in *Pot Black* and perhaps it is the simplicity of it all which has motivated its success.

One elderly lady may well have got somewhere near the mark when she wrote: 'The programme is full of nice-mannered people with smart bow ties.' Bow ties and good manners apart, *Pot Black* is an established favourite with viewers in three continents. Besides the fanatical following in the United Kingdom, it has also taken off in New Zealand, Hong Kong and Australia, where the programme's impact has exceeded all expectations. Australian champion Eddie Charlton, *Pot Black* champion in 1972, 1973 and 1980, says: 'The programme is compulsive viewing in Australia. Each series has been shown within a few weeks after the UK transmissions. *Pot Black* players are hero-worshipped here.'

To the players who are invited to appear in it, *Pot Black* means much more than the occasional television engagement. It accords them overseas exposure, extra bookings and increased earning-power. The programme 'discovered' and nurtured two young players in Graham Miles and Dennis Taylor, both of whom claim *Pot Black* has had a considerable effect on their livelihoods and standings in the professional ranks.

Technical hiccups aside, the biggest problem surrounding any *Pot Black* recording session concerns the allocation of tickets for the studio audience. Approximately 1500 people visit the Pebble Mill studios in Birmingham each December – six sessions with a capacity of 250 – many of whom have waited patiently on the ticket list for up to nearly a year! There are many more than 1500 disappointed fans whose written applications have been received after the list has been closed – nowadays by the end of March.

The first *Pot Black* competition ran for eight weeks and featured eight players in an 'instant death' knock-out competition. From 1970 onwards the series was extended to sixteen weeks and each series up to 1976 contained six or eight professionals. Various permutations have been employed to arrive at the required sixteen programmes, ensuring at the same time that both the viewer and the player understood the system!

It is not possible with eight players for them all to play each other even once, in sixteen weeks. Initially it would take twenty-eight weeks for this to happen. Four *Pot Black* Champions against four Challengers in two leagues has worked well, at least mathematically. This method was used in 1975 and 1976 and provided a *Pot Black* 'Champion' against a 'Challenger' in the Finals. (The runner-up in each year was Dennis Taylor.) Also in each competition there is a prize for the highest break of the series and since 1975 a special award – a replica of the *Pot Black* Trophy – has been presented to snooker personalities during the final ceremonies.

The 1977 series featured twelve players and included the first appearance of the left-handed South African

Perrie Mans, and the Welshman Doug Mountjoy. Mans was the reigning South African champion whereas Mountjoy had just turned professional after winning the World Amateur Championship in Mans' home town of Johannesburg. Coincidentally, it was these two players who found themselves competing in the Final, with Mans earning the title of *Pot Black* Champion 1977.

The programme celebrated its tenth birthday in 1978 and by the end of the fifteen-week series, won by Doug Mountjoy in a three-frame Final from Graham Miles, it had amassed an average viewing figure of three million viewers each week!

In 1979, the team of eight players included all six previous winners of the Trophy. Ray Reardon, the first *Pot Black* champion in 1969, won for the second time, against Doug Mountjoy in the three-frame Final. In the closing ceremonies, the actor Sir Ralph Richardson presented the Trophy, and a special prize – a decanter which had belonged to Joe Davis – was presented by his widow June for the highest break in the series.

Pot Black entered the eighties with another strong team of eight professionals: Ray Reardon, Doug Mountjoy, Dennis Taylor, Graham Miles, John Spencer, Perrie Mans, Eddie Charlton and the 1979 World Snooker Champion, Terry Griffiths. Reardon's attempt to win the Trophy for the third time failed when he was beaten in the three-frame Final by the Australian Eddie Charlton. The main prizes were presented by Cliff Morgan, OBE, the Head of BBC Outside Broadcasts Group, Television, and June Davis presented the Joe Davis Trophy to Dennis Taylor for his break of 87, the highest in the series. A delighted and very surprised Alan Weeks opened the envelope containing the name of the winner of the Personality Award – to discover that he himself was the recipient!

The selection of the eight players for 1981 was based on the quarter-finalists in the 1980 World Snooker Championships. Among them were two young Canadians, Kirk Stevens and Jim Wych, and the reigning World Champion, also from Canada, Cliff Thorburn, who competed with Ray Reardon, David Taylor, Alex Higgins, Eddie Charlton and Steve Davis.

For the first time in many years Sydney Lee, the programme's famous referee, was (due to ill-health) unable to officiate, and John Williams from Wrexham, the 'senior' referee, was invited to take over Syd's duties. The competition was dominated by the Canadians – the winner was Cliff Thorburn, the runner-up Jim Wych, and Kirk Stevens won the highest break prize with a score of 79. *Pot Black*'s Personality Award also went overseas – to Australia's Eddie Charlton. George Howard, Chairman of the BBC, presented the main prizes after a Final watched by over nine million viewers.

The 1982 series was notable on at least two not entirely unrelated counts: audience figures – an average of over eight million viewers a week was the largest in the programme's history; and the presence of the 1981 World Champion, Steve Davis, who, although he had previously played in the 1979 and 1981 series, had really captured the public's imagination by 1982. The Final featured the youngest and the oldest of the eight competitors, Steve Davis and Eddie Charlton, with Steve gaining his first *Pot Black* Championship by two frames to nil. The presentations were made by the Minister for Sport, Neil Macfarlane MP. Eddie Charlton, the runner-up, also won

Pot Black 1983. *Sydney Lee, the former referee, makes the presentation to Steve Davis, watched by Alan Weeks.*

the highest break prize with a score of 98. The two losing semi-finalists were Cliff Thorburn and Doug Mountjoy, and the 'non-qualifiers' were David Taylor, Dennis Taylor, Alex Higgins and Ray Reardon, who also won the Personality Award.

In the 1983 series two 'newcomers', Tony Knowles and Jimmy White, joined Eddie Charlton, Steve Davis, Alex Higgins, Ray Reardon, Kirk Stevens and Willie Thorne. Steve Davis beat Ray Reardon in the Final and also took the *Pot Black* Personality Award, while Ray won the highest break prize with a score of 91.

As the result of negotiations between the BBC and the WPBSA (the professional body), a new format was agreed for *Pot Black* 84. It meant that no less than sixteen players – double the usual number – competed in an 'instant death' one-frame knock-out event. The majority of them had qualified for the last sixteen of the 1983 World Championship and three players – the South African Silvino Francisco, Tony Meo and the Billiards Champion Mark Wildman – appeared in the series for the first time. Terry Griffiths, who had only played in the competition once before, in 1980, was the eventual 1984

Pot Black 1984. *Paul McGann, star of BBC TV's* Give Us a Break *presents the trophy to Terry Griffiths. Alan Weeks holds the cheque.*

Pot Black Champion, beating John Spencer 2–1 in the Final. Dennis Taylor won the highest break prize with a score of 81 and the *Pot Black* Personality Award was presented 'off-stage' to the programme's former producer, Reg Perrin. Paul McGann, star of BBC TV's *Give Us A Break*, awarded the main prizes.

Pot Black honours list

1969   Winner: Ray Reardon 88 – 29
        Runner-up: John Spencer
        Highest break in series: Ray Reardon (99)

1970   Winner: John Spencer 88 – 27
        Runner-up: Ray Reardon
        Highest break in series: Fred Davis (54)

1971   Winner: John Spencer 61 – 40
        Runner-up: Fred Davis
        Highest break in series: Fred Davis (73)

1972   Winner: Eddie Charlton 75 – 43
        Runner-up: Ray Reardon
        Highest break in series: John Spencer (66)

1973   Winner: Eddie Charlton 93 – 33
        Runner-up: Rex Williams

Highest break in series: Eddie Charlton (110)

1974   Winner: Graham Miles 77 – 37, 70 – 49
        Runner-up: John Spencer
        Highest break in series: Graham Miles (68)

1975   Winner: Graham Miles 81 – 27
        Runner-up: Dennis Taylor
        Highest break in series: Fred Davis (87)

1976   Winner: John Spencer 69 – 42
        Runner-up: Dennis Taylor
        Highest break in series: Eddie Charlton (64)

1977   Winner: Perrie Mans 90 – 21
        Runner-up: Doug Mountjoy
        Highest break in series: Perrie Mans (59)

1978   Winner: Doug Mountjoy 43 – 55, 97 – 23,
          111 – 16
        Runner-up: Graham Miles
        Highest break in series: Doug Mountjoy (101)

1979   Winner: Ray Reardon 79 – 51, 25 – 82, 84 – 41
        Runner-up: Doug Mountjoy
        Highest break in series: Doug Mountjoy (82)

1980   Winner: Eddie Charlton 16 – 74, 85 – 30,
          68 – 54
        Runner-up: Ray Reardon
        Highest break in series: Dennis Taylor (87)

1981   Winner: Cliff Thorburn 68 – 39, 85 – 50
        Runner-up: Jim Wych
        Highest break in series: Kirk Stevens (79)

1982   Winner: Steve Davis 82 – 40, 85 – 38
        Runner-up: Eddie Charlton
        Highest break in series: Eddie Charlton (98)

1983   Winner: Steve Davis 61 – 60, 82 – 47
        Runner-up: Ray Reardon
        Highest break in series: Ray Reardon (91)

1984   Winner: Terry Griffiths 57 – 65, 77 – 8, 70 – 35
        Runner-up: John Spencer
        Highest break in series: Dennis Taylor (81)

Televising Snooker
by Nick Hunter

In 1976 the Embassy World Snooker Championship was held half in Manchester, half in Middlesbrough. Some forty-five minutes of snooker were transmitted on *Grandstand*. There were severe problems with the promotion. The finalists were extremely unhappy with the television lighting, and at one stage threatened not to play. The fact that Ray Reardon beat Alex Higgins and won £6000 went almost unnoticed by a small TV audience, and the recriminations that went on afterwards affected the whole world of snooker.

In 1984 the very same event was held entirely at the Crucible in Sheffield. More than 100 hours of snooker were transmitted by the BBC over the seventeen-day event; the TV audience reached nearly fourteen million. Steve Davis's victory was front-page news, and the £40,000 he won was but a drop in the ocean compared with the real promotional value of that win in an unforgettable Final against Jimmy White.

In the nine years that span those two Championships – even allowing for inflation! – it is clear that a revolution has occurred. The worried dozen or so professionals who met in the early seventies and decided to put up their own money 'to keep the World Championship alive' can be compared with the 100 plus professionals who now see millions of pounds from television and sponsors flowing into the game's coffers.

The story really goes back beyond 1976 – to 1969, when Philip Lewis, who was then the BBC's sports producer in Birmingham, was the first person in television to realise that colour meant that the game could now not only be understood on television but was also pretty to watch! The result? *Pot Black*.

Pot Black laid the foundations for the 'snooker boom'. John Spencer, Eddie Charlton, Ray Reardon, and Alex Higgins were already well known in 1976, when I returned to the game. I had earlier come into contact with

Messrs Pulman, Williams and Fred Davis in a black-and-white *Grandstand* challenge match in 1967. It was one 'live' frame between each of three horse-races. 'No longer than seventeen minutes a frame', I was told. The players obliged. While I applauded their professionalism and the way they could play a frame against the clock, the greys and blacks did not seem to me to herald a TV sport with much of a future. All of this seems a long time ago. Players are now recognised the world over, they even write their 'memoirs' at the tender age of twenty or thirty, and some of those reminiscences are actually about snooker!

One half of the 1976 World Championship, including the Final, was held at the Wythenshawe Forum in Manchester. I had gone down there several times during the previous week to check up on some technical details, meet the organisers and watch the snooker. The snooker I saw was riveting. Alex Higgins was doing his Houdini act against John Spencer and Cliff Thorburn, and the Forum's roof was in grave danger of collapse! I had never realised that snooker could be like that, people cheering and clapping and sitting on the edge of their seats hardly daring to breathe. With respect to *Pot Black*, I thought that tournament snooker with its tactics and increased suspense was an even better bet for television, and given that many of the players were already well known to the public, then TV should be showing much more of the Championship than the last few frames of the Final.

You can imagine my feelings when I discovered a few days later that the Reardon/Higgins Final was becoming a very one-sided affair, and that Reardon himself was not going to continue unless we altered our lighting! In those days television came in during the Final and we only broadcast the last session. So the players began with the traditional shade, and finished with the television lighting. However the lighting was arranged, there would be problems as the lighting 'level' was bound to be very different. Television lighting changed the whole feel of the game as far as the players are concerned.

We did not realise, in those days, that shining lights on a snooker table could make so much difference to the players. So long as we weren't blinding them, all we had to worry about was the lighting level for the cameras, we thought. When Ray Reardon found he could not see the object-ball clearly, and had difficulty seeing the angles around the table, he quite understandably protested. It was clear that we needed to do some homework to sort out these conditions: the players deserved the best; our programmes would be better if the conditions were right. I suppose the biggest technical improvement since 1976 is in the lighting and we have worked very hard to try and make the television conditions as perfect as we can. Mike Watterson, the promoter, John Crowther, one of the BBC's engineering managers in Manchester, and I, spent the next couple of years gradually improving the player's lot. We feel we have just about solved the problems.

Very briefly, the main difficulty was that when the player is lit sitting down or standing back from the table – and I was very keen on these reaction shots being available – the lights reflecting in the balls acted as though a gauze curtain had been drawn between the player and the balls on the table. Every light source above and to the side of the table gives one reflection in each of the balls – sixty lamps, sixty reflections. If those reflections get towards the centre of the balls, then it becomes impossible to judge distance and direction accurately. This is what Ray Reardon objected to in 1976.

After some studio tests we devised a system of hiding the offending lamps from the table by using a sort of skirt. I could get my close-ups, the players could see what they were doing. Eureka! We celebrated too soon. In 1978, at the Crucible, a lamp burst and nearly showered the 'Hurricane' with white-hot filament! The new TV lighting rig was then taken to Wales and promptly made a hole in the cloth after another lamp had burst. We also knew that a long match played under these lamps made the players very hot and tired, and that in a long Championship they could lose many pounds in weight; and that the table became more like a skating rink as the cloth dried out. Once again John Crowther came to the rescue with a strip lighting rig – much less heat and it does not burn holes in the cloth, or Alex Higgins! That is the television lighting rig that many players now actually prefer to the shade.

From the player's point of view the television lighting has made a colossal difference. The shade illuminated the table and nothing else; the audience was heard but not seen; the player was in his own world, punctuated by applause he could hear but not see. Television removes the shade, and at the same time greatly increases the lighting level. The result is that the audience is very much in the player's view and the private world of the snooker player is now public. Concentration becomes far more difficult, and he feels the eyes of the public, he sees the smiles, he notices the movement. Most of my readers will have seen how all this affects some of the players: some thrive on it, some can't play well without it, some fall to pieces because of it.

To the casual viewer, snooker would appear to be a simple game to televise. Everything is contained in a small area – not like the Grand National where twenty cameras are needed, not like a Grand Prix where cars capable of near 200 miles an hour career round an undulating 2–3-mile course, not like a Test Match where a cricket ball can be propelled at 100 miles an hour and despatched by a desperate batsman in the opposite direction from that which he intended! True, but as we have discovered, snooker has its own particular problems, and woe betide the producer or director who decides it's all too easy!

The director's job is to make sure the viewer sees everything in the same quiet and relaxed manner in which snooker is being played. If the director gets it right then what he is doing will not be noticed. It is possible to ruin snooker with over-fussy direction, which only ends up by frustrating and finally infuriating the viewer. In snooker the director has time to think. It's the time to think that can create the problems.

All this of course is paralleled in the commentary box, except the commentator has to cope with both the expert viewer and the viewer new to the game – and thank goodness there are millions of them! He also does not always know which of his remarks are being transmitted – we still record most of our snooker. I well remember one unfortunate commentator who was understandably annoyed when a highlights programme, containing bits of four frames, included the same observation four times over and resulted in a number of insulting viewers' letters. As some of the players have found out when they have 'guested' in the commentary box, it's not as easy as it sounds! One well-known player couldn't utter a word, and sat in the chair speechless for two frames.

The television presence in the playing area is intense. Two cameras are positioned at each black pocket at ground-floor level, presiding over the proceedings like prehistoric monsters! The cameramen try not to move, but the cameras take some getting used to. One player once told me that as he played a shot he saw the lens move as the cameraman zoomed! His concentration had clearly been affected. The main two cameras are twenty or so feet above the table – and this is why the shade has to go, to enable these cameras to see the whole table.

All television staff at the major tournaments need stamina and concentration. At Sheffield, for instance, with some 300 hours of snooker recorded, 100 or so hours of transmission, and seventeen days of working some fifteen hours a day, we also need strong constitutions! It is easily the longest annual event of any description that the BBC covers. Without being dramatic about it, it only requires one slip and there's David Vine holding the fort!

Not that viewers don't enjoy our embarrassment! On one never-to-be-forgotten occasion we tried to transmit a Ray Reardon century break we had recorded earlier. David Vine introduced the frame that was supposed to last about twelve minutes, and there was Ray Reardon studying a table with twenty-one coloured balls in position. He potted a red, and with horrified eyes I saw the same Ray Reardon looking at just the final black! All this had taken precisely fifteen seconds. We had absolutely nothing to fall back on other than the unfortunate but nearly imperturbable David Vine who in the end talked to the camera for some five minutes with all around him in chaos. He even suggested the viewers should have a cup of tea . . . . Thankfully, such a happening is rare and is always the product of several mistakes all made at the same time. This story is related in the fervent hope that nothing like it happens again! We want to entertain our viewers, but with the snooker, not our own shortcomings.

Just as a snooker player, tired and under pressure, can make mistakes, so, of course, can we. The World Championship in particular is a real marathon for the production team, but most of us agree that there is only one day we are not looking forward to the following year, and that is the day after it finishes.

One other effect television has had is to shorten the matches in the World Championship. These were often played over seventy-odd or even over 100 frames – too indigestible for television. Viewers would not sit in front of their sets in large numbers for a week or more to watch

The World Championship scene.

one match. I think, and hope, that the longest match of all, the 35-frame Final of the World Championship, does mean that the best player wins, although I know some of the professionals prefer even longer matches. I respect their view but I hope they also respect the reason why the distances are relatively shorter. One of the most impressive facts about Steve Davis's extraordinary record over the last few years is that he has won *all* the tournaments between *Pot Black*'s one-frame format, and the long-distance World Championship, where *all* matches are over at least nineteen frames.

Since 1976 snooker coverage on television has been completely changed. The lighting, the camera positions, the transmission times are all quite different. Ted Lowe remains, and how grateful I've been for his advice. Ted taught me, along with the players, that if you treated snooker as a minor sport, then you won't get it right.

The World Championship was moved to the Crucible Theatre in Sheffield for 1977 with – crucially – the whole tournament taking place under one roof. There was extended coverage from the semi-finals onwards and there would have been more but for a mix-up in dates. After their traumatic experiences behind the scenes in 1976 Peter Dyke and Embassy kept faith with the Championship. 1978 and 1979 were the really exciting years for us. Daily coverage saw fan mail, telegrams and flowers arriving for the players. The citizens of Sheffield started gathering outside the Crucible's stage door to watch the players arrive. Best of all, for us in the BBC, the viewing figures started to rise, and kept on rising. They were heady days. Everyone involved with the Championship, everyone who had believed in snooker as a box-office attraction, knew they were being proved right.

It will be largely up to the players to ensure that this upward trend is maintained. All the players I know are rightly jealous of the standards they have set and, in particular, the spirit in which snooker is played. As far as I am concerned, we in television would have to try very hard to spoil the drama and excitement we have enjoyed so much over the years.

As night follows day, so television was going to affect snooker, like any marriage for better or for worse – and certainly for richer! I believe, so far, the pluses far outweigh the minuses. In 1976 the snooker world largely consisted of *Pot Black*, the Benson and Hedges, and three-quarters of an hour of highlights of the World Championship. There were not many of the twenty or so playing professionals who could live off the game. Nowadays the bulk of the top fifty of the 100 plus players are able to eke out a living 'potting balls' in the eight major televised tournaments and the handful of regional events covered by television. There are plenty of individual sponsors more than interested in linking their names with players of a sport that has such an enviable image of skill and sportsmanship, good manners and sartorial elegance.

The Rules of Snooker

Authorised by the Billiards and Snooker Control Council

1
Definition
of Game

The game of *Snooker* (or Snooker's Pool) is played on an English Billiard Table, and may be played by two or more persons, either as sides, or independently. It is a game of winning hazards; cannons are ignored. The winner is the player or side making the highest score, or to whom the game, under Rule 14, is awarded.

The balls

2
Number
in set

The set of balls should be twenty-two in number, consisting of fifteen reds, one black, one pink, one blue, one brown, one green, one yellow and a white ball, which is called the cue-ball. In the game on the B. & S. C. C. 6 ft. Standard Table the set of balls shall be seventeen in number, consisting of ten reds, one black, one pink, one blue, one brown, one green, one yellow and a white ball, which is called the cue-ball.

Technical terms

3 a

The white ball is referred to as the *cue-ball*; the yellow, green, brown, blue, pink and black, as the *pool balls*, or *colours*, the red (or pyramid) balls as *reds*.

b
Ball forced
off Table

Any ball which is forced off the table becomes out of play, but, with the exception of a red ball, is immediately replaced upon its allotted spot.

c
Ball 'On'
To Play at
Balls

A player is said to be *on* a ball when such ball may be lawfully struck by the cue-ball under these Rules. He is *on* a pool ball nominated under Rules 5 and 10.

d
Player
Snookered

A player is said to be *snookered* with regard to any ball when a direct stroke in a straight line of the cue-ball to any point of such ball is obstructed by any ball which is not *on*. If a player is *in hand* after a foul, he cannot be *snookered* with regard to any ball that is *on*, if he can get a direct stroke in a straight line from some part of the 'D' (*i.e.*, a clear ball).

When the ball *on* is snookered by more than one ball, the effective snookering ball is the one nearest to the cue-ball.

e
Cue-ball Angled
The cue-ball is said to be *angled* when the corner of the cushion prevents a stroke being made, in a straight line, directly on any part of any ball that may be lawfully struck.

f
Nominated Ball
A *Nominated Ball* is the object-ball which the striker declares he undertakes to strike with the first impact of the cue-ball.

4
Placing the Balls
Fifteen reds in the form of a triangle, the ball at the apex standing as near to the pink ball as possible, without touching it; the base being parallel with and nearest to the top cushion: BLACK on the BILLIARD SPOT; PINK on the PYRAMID SPOT; BLUE on the CENTRE SPOT; BROWN on the MIDDLE of the baulk-line; GREEN on the LEFT-HAND and YELLOW on the RIGHT-HAND corner of the 'D'.

5
Mode of Play

First Stroke

Cue-Ball Pocketed

Re-spotting the Balls
Last Red

Pocketing Pool Balls

Nominating
Players must first determine by lot, or other convenient method, the order of their turn, which must remain unaltered throughout the game. The first player shall play from hand. The cue-ball shall strike a red as the initial stroke of each turn, until all the reds are off the table. The value of each red, lawfully pocketed by the same stroke, is scored. For the next stroke of the turn (if a score is made) the cue-ball shall strike a pool ball, the value of which (if lawfully pocketed) is scored. The game is continued by pocketing reds, and pool balls, alternately, in the same turn. If the striker fails to score, the player next in turn plays from where the cue-ball came to rest. If the cue-ball is pocketed or forced off the table, the next player plays from hand. Once the cue-ball has come to rest on the table after a foul has been committed it must be played from where it has come to rest. Each *pool ball* pocketed or forced off the table must be re-spotted before the next stroke, until finally pocketed under these Rules. If the player who lawfully pockets the last red, pocket any pool ball with his next stroke, this ball is re-spotted. Otherwise (reds being off the table) the pool balls must be struck by the cue-ball in the progressive order of their values and *if lawfully pocketed* are not re-spotted. When requested by the referee a player must state which ball he

Intentional Miss	is *on*. He is advised to do so for his own protection. An intentional miss shall not be made. The player shall, to the best of his ability, endeavour to strike a ball that is *on*.
First Impact	The first impact of the cue-ball shall govern all strokes.
EXAMPLE	A player *on* blue makes the first impact with the cue-ball on the blue, the cue-ball then strikes the black or any other ball and goes into a pocket the player is penalised five points, the value of the blue, the ball on which the cue-ball made the first impact.
6 *Ball Values*	The scoring values of the balls are: red—1, yellow—2, green—3, brown—4, blue—5, pink—6, black—7.
7 *Re-spotting Pool Balls*	The striker must see that every ball required to be re-spotted is properly placed before he plays his stroke. *Reds* are never re-spotted. Any pool ball pocketed by a foul stroke is not deemed to have been lawfully pocketed, and shall be re-spotted. If the spot, named in Rule 4 for each pool ball, is occupied when such ball shall be placed thereon, the ball shall be placed on the spot first named in Rule 4, that is then unoccupied, i.e., if the spot allocated to the yellow is occupied by another ball, after the yellow has been pocketed, then the yellow ball is to be placed on the black spot, or, if that is occupied, then on the pink spot, and so on. If all the spots are occupied, any pool ball other than the black and pink shall be placed as near its own spot as possible between that spot and the *nearest part* of the top cushion without touching another ball. In the case of the black and pink balls being potted and all the spots are occupied, they shall be placed as near as possible to their own spots, up the table, on the centre line of the table, and without touching another ball. If the space between the black spot and the top cushion is occupied, the black ball shall be placed as near as possible to the black spot, on the centre line of the table, below its spot, and without touching another ball. Similarly if the space between the pink spot and the top cushion is occupied, the pink shall be placed as near as possible to the pink spot, on the centre line of the table, below its spot, and without touching another ball.

31

Balls struck simultaneously or pocketed on one stroke

Two balls (other than two reds or the ball 'on' and the ball nominated under Rule 10) must not be struck simultaneously nor pocketed by the same stroke.

NOTE

Any number of red balls may be pocketed by one stroke made in accordance with these rules.

9 a
Cue-ball Touching

If the cue-ball is touching another ball which is *on*, the striker must play away from the touching ball without moving the latter, or he must be held to have pushed. The striker thus playing away from a ball *on* shall incur no penalty for a miss or for striking another ball, but he may lawfully pocket any other ball which is *on*. If he pockets a ball which is not *on*, he forfeits the penalty under Rule 12

b

If the cue-ball is touching another ball which is not *on*, the striker must play away from such ball as in (a). If the ball *on* is missed, or another ball hit, the penalty as laid down in Rule 12 must be forfeited.

c

In all cases where the cue-ball is touching the ball *on* or touching a colour after a red has been potted, the referee shall state 'TOUCHING BALL' without being asked. If the cue-ball is touching more than one ball 'on' he shall, on request, state which ball(s) the cue-ball is touching. He shall offer no other information.

EXAMPLES

(1)

The *ball on is red*, cue-ball is *touching red*, striker plays away from red without disturbing it, strikes and goes in off black. The penalty is four points, the value of the ball *on*.

(2)

The *ball on is yellow*, cue-ball is *touching yellow*, striker plays away from yellow without disturbing it and pockets black. The penalty is seven points, the value of the ball *pocketed*.

(3)

The *ball on is red*, cue-ball is *touching black*, striker plays away from black without disturbing it, misses all balls and cue-ball enters a pocket. The penalty is four points, the value of the ball *on*.

(4)

In the case of the striker, playing away from black, missing all reds and striking blue he is penalised five points.

10
Snookering After a foul

After a foul stroke, if the striker be snookered (a) *with regard to all reds* he is then *on* any ball he may nominate, and for all purposes such nominated ball shall be regarded as a red, except that, if pocketed, it shall be spotted; (b) After a foul stroke, if the striker be snookered, (*reds being off the table*) *with regard to the pool ball on*, he is then *on* any ball he may nominate, and for all purposes such nominated ball shall be regarded as the ball *on*, except that should it be lawfully pocketed it shall be spotted, and the player shall continue his break on the ball he was *on*, but for being snookered. If, as a result of playing on the nominated ball, the ball *on* be pocketed, it shall be scored and the player continues his break.

Nominated Ball

Nominated Ball and Ball 'on' Pocketed

Should both the nominated ball and the ball *on* be pocketed by the same stroke, only the ball *on* shall be scored, and the player continues his break. The nominated ball only shall be re-spotted.

Snookered by the Nominated ball

Should the striker leave the opponent snookered by the nominated ball it is a foul stroke, except when only pink and black remain on the table.

Missing the ball Nominated

Should the striker fail to hit the ball nominated under this Rule it is a foul stroke.

11
Cue-ball Angled

If the cue-ball is angled it must be played from where it lies; but if angled after a foul, it may be played from hand, at the striker's discretion.

12
Penalties

A player who contravenes any Rule of this game: (a) cannot score; (b) loses his turn; (c) forfeits such points as are exacted in these Rules— which are added to his opponent's score; (d) in addition, the striker has the option of playing from where the balls have come to rest, or requesting the opponent to play the stroke; (e) minimum penalty for any infringement is four points.

13
Foul Strokes

The player contravenes these rules by the following acts (among others):

a   By making a losing hazard. Penalty, value of ball *on*, or value of ball struck, whichever is the higher.

b   By causing the cue-ball to strike a ball he is not *on*. Penalty, value of the ball struck, or value of the ball *on*, whichever is the higher.

c   By making a miss. Penalty, value of the ball *on*.

d   By snookering his opponent with the nominated ball after a foul stroke, except when only pink and black remain. Penalty, value of the ball *on*.

e   By striking simultaneously or pocketing with one stroke two balls, except two reds, or the ball *on* and the ball nominated. Penalty, highest value of the two struck, or pocketed.

f   By moving an object-ball in contravention of Rule 9. (Cue-ball Touching.) Penalty, value of the ball *on*, or value of the ball moved, whichever is the higher.

g   By forcing a ball off the table. Penalty, the value of the ball *on*, or value of the ball forced off the table, whichever is the higher.

h   By pocketing any ball not *on*. Penalty, value of the ball *pocketed*, or value of the ball *on*, whichever is the higher.

i   For playing with other than the cue-ball. Penalty seven points.

j   By playing at two reds in successive strokes. Penalty, seven points.

k   By using a dead ball to test whether a ball will pass another, or go on a spot, for any other purpose. Penalty, seven points.

l   By playing with both feet off the floor. Penalty, value of the ball *on*, or value of the ball struck, or value of the ball pocketed or value of the ball improperly spotted, whichever is the higher.

m   By playing before the balls have come to rest, or before they have been spotted or when wrongly spotted. Penalty, value of the ball *on*, or value of the ball struck, or value of the ball wrongly spotted, or value of the ball pocketed, whichever is the higher.

n   By striking or touching a ball whilst in play, otherwise than with the tip of the cue. Penalty, value of the *ball struck* or *touched*, or value of the ball *on*, whichever is the higher.

o   By playing improperly from hand. Penalty, value of the ball *on*, or value of the ball struck, or value of the ball pocketed, or value of the ball improperly spotted, whichever is the higher.

p   Push Stroke. Penalty, value of the ball *on*, or value of the ball struck, or value of the ball pocketed, whichever is the higher.

q   Jump Shot. Penalty, value of the ball *on*, or value of the ball struck, or value of the ball pocketed, whichever is the higher.

r   By playing out of turn. Penalty, value of the ball *on*, or value of the ball struck, or value of the ball pocketed, whichever is the higher.

s   Failing to nominate when awarded a free ball, penalty to be the value of the ball struck, or value of the ball pocketed, or if no ball is struck, the value of the ball *on*.

Only the referee is allowed to clean a ball on the table. He should do so at a player's request.

It is the striker's responsibility to see that the balls are correctly spotted before playing his stroke.

If the referee considers that a player is taking an abnormal amount of time over his stroke, with the intention of upsetting his opponent, the referee should warn him that he runs the risk of being disqualified if he pursues these tactics.

A player should not be penalised if, when using the rest, the rest head falls off and touches a ball.

Unless a foul stroke is awarded by the referee, or claimed by the non-striker, before the next stroke is made, it is condoned.

If the striker plays with the balls improperly spotted, he scores all points made until the foul is awarded by the referee, or claimed by the non-striker.

The referee should not give any indication that a player is about to make a foul stroke.

If the striker makes a miss, the referee can order him to re-play the stroke penalising him the requisite forfeit for each miss, but he scores all points in any subsequent stroke.

When snookered after a foul stroke, a player must nominate the ball he intends to play.

If at the opening stroke of a game the striker fails to hit a red, the next player plays from where the cue-ball has come to rest.

A Snooker A player must be able to strike both sides of the ball *on* free of obstruction from any ball or balls not *on*. It virtually means the diameter of a ball on either side of the ball *on*.

If a player is colour blind, the referee should tell him the colour of a ball if requested.

A referee must declare when a player has a free ball without appeal from a player.

Examples of (1) *Red is the ball on*, striker fouls *the black* with
Foul Strokes his cue or otherwise, the penalty is seven points, the value of the *ball fouled*.
(2) *Black is the ball on*, striker fouls *a red* with his cue or arm, the penalty is seven points, the value of the *ball on*.
(3) A player pots the *pink* and before it is

35

properly spotted he pots a *red* ball – what is the penalty?

Decision: six points for playing with the balls not properly spotted (value of the ball not properly spotted).

Wilful Evasion of
Spirit of Rules

If a game is awarded to a player under Rule 15 GENERAL RULES, the offender shall lose the game, and forfeit all points he may have scored, or the value of the balls on the table (reds = 8 each) whichever is higher.

14
End of Game
and Tie

When only the black ball is left, the first score or forfeit ends the game, unless the scores are then equal, in which case the black is spotted, and the players draw lots for choice of playing at the black from hand. The next score or forfeit ends the game. In games (whether individuals, pairs or teams) where aggregate points decide the winner, it is only when the scores are equal *AS A RESULT OF THE LAST FRAME*, that the black is re-spotted. The next score or forfeit ends the game.

RULE CHANGE

As from 1 December 1973, players will not be required to nominate their colour when taking a free ball unless there is doubt over which ball the player is attempting.

Pot Black Postbag

During *Pot Black*'s sixteen-week run there is always a very heavy load of correspondence from viewers. Apart from those commenting, favourably or otherwise, on the programmes, many viewers use *Pot Black* as an Advice Bureau, and deluge us with questions, the answers to which often demand a certain amount of ingenuity, not to mention research. The questions vary a lot, but the most popular, even though we have given the answer on the air in an attempt to reduce the postbag, concerns the highest break a player can achieve in snooker. This particular query will in time become a classic at any snooker quiz. So what is the answer? A break of 155 is technically possible, which would come about if a foul stroke was committed at the break-off. This would give the opponent a free ball counting as a red (one point) and by taking the black he could add 8 points to the accepted maximum break of 147. As far as is known, no player has ever achieved a break of 155, and so for obvious reasons the maximum break is recognised by the world governing body as 147.

Now let us look at what I would describe as being typical *Pot Black* posers.

Q Is it a foul stroke if, when commencing a game, the striker fails to strike a red?

A It is 4 away and the opponent takes his turn from where the cue-ball has come to rest.

Q Is it a foul shot if a player strikes a cushion before hitting the red at the opening stroke of the game?

A No.

Q In a match of more than one frame does the player who has potted the black in the previous game break off in the next frame?

A Not necessarily so. The break should run alternately and be decided by the spin of a coin when an odd number of games are played.

37

Q When addressing the cue-ball at the opening stroke of the game the player accidentally touches the ball with the tip of his cue. Can he replace the ball and play again or does he play the cue-ball from the position where it had come to rest?

A At the slightest touch of the ball the player must leave the table and allow his opponent to play from where the cue-ball has come to rest. There is also a penalty of 4 points.

Q Is the player allowed to play the cue-ball against a cushion without making an attempt to hit the pack of reds at the opening stroke of the game?

A Definitely no. He must at all times make an attempt to strike the 'ball on'.

Q What is the penalty if a player plays his shot with both feet off the floor?

A The penalty is the value of the 'ball on'.

Q Is there any penalty when the striker's tie, coat, shirt sleeve, or any other part of his person touches a ball, even though it does not move it?

A Yes, the penalty is the value of the 'ball on', or the value of the ball touched if it is of higher value.

Q What is the penalty when the cue-ball is forced off the table?

A It is the value of the 'ball on' and the next player plays from the D.

Q What is the penalty when the cue-ball and object-ball are forced off the table?

A Again, the value of the 'ball on', and if it is a coloured ball it is respotted.

Q What is the position if a player pockets more than one red by the same stroke?

A One point is scored for each red pocketed.

Q Player on a red strikes it, then cannons on to the black, or another colour, and runs into a pocket. Is the penalty 4 or 7 points?

A The penalty is only 4 points.

Q Player on a red strikes it, then cannons on to the black, or any other colour, which falls into a pocket. What is the penalty?

A   In this case the penalty is a minimum of 4 points unless the colour potted is of higher value, when it is the value of the colour potted.

Q   After potting a red ball is the player allowed to roll the cue-ball behind a coloured ball leaving a deliberate snooker?

A   Yes, this move is a fair shot.

Q   After potting a red a player inadvertently pockets another red instead of a colour. What is the penalty?

A   It is 7 away. The highest valued ball on the table.

Q   Having potted a coloured ball the striker inadvertently pots another colour. How many points are forfeited?

A   Four points or the value of the second colour potted, if higher.

Q   Striker misses the pack of red balls which is a foul stroke giving 4 away. His opponent is not actually snookered, but he cannot strike any particular red on either extreme edge. Can he claim a free ball?

A   You cannot claim a free ball if you are only prevented from striking both sides of a 'ball on' by the intervention of another 'ball on' or a cushion.

Q   My opponent having gone 'in off' a red leaves me in position that I cannot strike the 'ball on' full in the face *from any part* of the D. Can I claim to be snookered and have a free ball?

A   Definitely a free ball when you *cannot* strike the 'ball on' at any point from any part of the D.

Q   What is a free ball?

A   A player snookered after a foul shot by his opponent may nominate to play any coloured ball (a 'free ball'). If reds are still on the table, the nominated ball, if potted, counts one point (as a red). If the nominated (free) ball is potted and there are no reds left on the table, the score is the value of the lowest colour left on the table.

Q   What is a plant?

A   A position where two (or more) object-balls are played on to each other so that the second (or last) object-ball is potted.

Pot (Black) Pourri

DID YOU KNOW THAT ...

The technical adviser and 'trick-shot' player in the BBC TV series *Give Us A Break* was the Ealing professional Geoff Foulds?

Mike Watterson, promoter of the 1983 Jameson International and competitor, beat Perrie Mans and Tony Meo during the tournament?

National Snooker Championships have been held regularly in Iceland since 1929?

Eddie Charlton was the runner-up in the 1984 World Billiards Championship?

Ray Reardon, as PC 184, won the United Kingdom Police Championship four times?

Doug French, the 1983 Greenall Whitley Champion, was once a stand-up comic?

A Birmingham manufacturer of special snooker spectacles has called them the 'Cue' and the 'Cannon'?

South African champion Perrie Mans' hobbies include racing cars and racing pigeons?

On average, a new snooker club is being opened in the UK every week?

The official minimum length of a snooker cue is three feet?

In 1955 the World Snooker Championship was held in the Tower Circus, Blackpool?

Four snooker theme-tunes, including *Pot Black*'s 'Black and White Rag', are available on a BBC EP?

Steve Davis and Terry Griffiths drew 6–6 against Americans Jim Rempe and Mike Sigel in a snooker/pool challenge match in the Americas Hotel, Dallas?

DID YOU KNOW THAT . . .

The Association of Snooker Writers voted Bill Werbeniuk 'Personality of the Year' in 1983?

One of the tables at Hounslow Conservative Club was originally installed at Buckingham Palace in 1842 for Queen Victoria?

Pot Black commentator Ted Lowe's own story, *Between Frames*, was published in April 1984?

Wales won the Home International Amateur Snooker Championship for the fourth year running in 1983?

The first billiard table with a slate bed was delivered to White's Club, London, in 1826?

In 1983 eighteen players were granted professional status by the WPBSA, including Paul Mifsud from Malta?

The late Walter Lindrum's cue was bought at a London auction for £130?

The first Canadian to enter the World Snooker Championship was Con Stanbury in 1935?

Cliff Thorburn was decorated with the OBC (Order of Canada) for his services to snooker in Ottawa in April 1984?

Spain's first snooker centre, in Fuengirola, was opened in 1983?

Sixteen-year-old Allison Fisher from Peacehaven won the East Sussex Under 25 Championship and the individual championship of the Lewes League competing against men in both events?

The 1984 English Amateur Champion, Steve Longworth, and the runner-up, Wayne Jones, are now professionals?

Pot Black: Personalities and tips from the top

Eddie Charlton

Born in Merewether, New South Wales, on 31 October 1929, Eddie lived most of his life in Swansea, a coal-mining and fishing area ninety miles north of Sydney, where his grandfather had a small three-table billiard saloon. Eddie started playing about the age of nine, and by his eleventh birthday he could beat anybody in town.

In 1940 Walter Lindrum heard of Eddie's prowess and wrote to his grandfather asking him to bring Eddie to Sydney to play an exhibition. The invitation was accepted and Eddie played Walter one afternoon before a crowd of approximately 600 people, and that really was the commencement of the billiard and snooker career of Eddie Charlton. Eddie continued his education at his local secondary school in Swansea and then became a trainee apprentice fitter in the coal-mining industry.

Eddie completed twenty-two years in the coal mines in the New South Wales coalfield, and for all that time played soccer, the last twelve years First Division. For a similar period he joined in the Surf Life Saving Movement which meant that he virtually trained hard all winter and summer for those twenty-two years. 'I was so fit in those days it frightens me to think back on it compared with today.'

One of the highlights in his surfing career was to be a member of the Swansea Belmont Senior Surf Boat crew who won the Australian title in 1950 at Coolangatta, Queensland. During this time he also played 'A' grade tennis, 'A' reserve grade cricket, golf, squash, and through his amateur boxing career managed to win three amateur boxing titles and had the pleasure of boxing in four exhibitions with the late Dave Sands. Eddie was also a member of an athletic club and when the Olympic Games were held in Melbourne in 1956 the Olympic flame, having been flown from Greece to Darwin, was carried by runners over 3000 miles to Melbourne. Each runner carried the torch one mile. Eddie's brother Jim carried it the mile into Swansea and Eddie the mile out of Swansea. He still feels that this was one of the most exciting activities of his sporting career.

As an amateur he won three New South Wales State snooker titles and one New South Wales billiards title. He turned professional in 1960 and has held the Australian professional snooker title each year but one.

Among the titles he has held are: New South Wales Open Snooker Championship; New South Wales Professional Snooker Championship; Australian Professional Snooker Championship; Australian Match Play Snooker Championship; Australian Open Snooker Championship; British Commonwealth Open Snooker Championship; *Pot Black* Champion 1972, 1973 and 1980.

In the first of his attempts at the World Professional Snooker title he was beaten by John Pulman in the 1968 Final. In 1970 he was beaten in the semi-final, 1972 again beaten in a semi-final, 1973 beaten in the Final by Ray Reardon. Surprisingly, in 1974 he failed to reach the quarter-finals, but with the 1975 World Championship being played virtually on his doorstep, the Australian came within one frame of taking the title from Ray Reardon. In 1976 Eddie lost to Alex Higgins in the semi-finals, and later unsuccessfully challenged Rex Williams for the World Billiards title. At Sheffield in the 1977 World Championship he met the Canadian Champion, Cliff Thorburn, in the quarter-finals and lost by just one frame, 13–12. Twelve months later the same two players met again in the quarter-finals and on this occasion the result and the score were reversed when Eddie beat Cliff by the odd frame. However, his hope of reaching the Final disappeared when Ray Reardon defeated him by 18 frames to 14 in the semi-finals.

Since entering the World Championship in 1968, Eddie has often been involved in the closing stages. In 1979 he survived until the semi-finals, beating Doug Mountjoy and Fred Davis, but losing then to Terry Griffiths, who was to become the new World Champion, by only 19 frames to 17. Consolation for Eddie followed when he beat John Virgo in the 13-frame 'play-off' for third place. In the 1980 World Championship, after beating John Virgo again in the second round, he lost in the quarter-finals by 13–7 to the young Canadian Kirk Stevens.

Eddie has sacrificed Christmas in the Australian sunshine since 1972 to play in *Pot Black* (the programme is recorded just after Christmas). His efforts have been rewarded as he won the *Pot Black* Trophy for the third time in 1980, and no one has yet bettered his highest break in the series of 110, which he achieved in 1973.

At home in Sydney, Eddie combines playing with the management of a successful billiards company and the organisation of tournaments. He is the author of two books on snooker and, as one of the most popular players in *Pot Black*, his appearances have contributed to the success of the television series both in Australia and New Zealand. His contributions to the success of *Pot Black* were gratefully recognised in 1981 when he received the Personality Award – a silver replica of the *Pot Black* Trophy. Later in the year he failed to win his second-round game against Doug Mountjoy in the World Championship but made a welcome return visit to the Pebble Mill studios shortly afterwards. There Eddie presented the new *Junior Pot Black* Trophy to the winner, eighteen-year-old Dean Reynolds from Grimsby.

The Australian trio of Charlton (captain), Ian Anderson and Paddy Morgan, lost to England 4–3 (after a tie-break frame) and to Northern Ireland by 4–1 in the 1981 State

Express World Team Classic at the Hexagon Theatre, Reading. Eddie returned to Pebble Mill, Birmingham, in December 1981 to compete in his eleventh consecutive *Pot Black*. It was also to be his fourth appearance in the Final, but he was runner-up on this occasion to the 1981 World Champion Steve Davis. Eddie won the highest break prize for the third time, with a score of 98. In the 1982 Benson and Hedges Masters the Australian was beaten 5–1 by Alex Higgins in the quarter-finals, and his next major tournament was the World Championship. He has always tried extremely hard to win this title and once again reached the semi-finals. Ray Reardon – the man who had beaten Eddie in the 1973 and 1975 finals – was, yet again, to bring Eddie's chances to an end for another year, by 16 frames to 11.

Eddie's team of himself, Ian Anderson and Paddy Morgan lost to both Canada and Wales in the 1982 State Express Classic where Eddie had the only Australian individual success, beating Terry Griffiths 2–1. He was beaten by another Welshman, Ray Reardon, in the 1983 *Pot Black* semi-finals, and by Steve Davis in the Lada Classic quarter-finals. In the 1983 Benson and Hedges Masters, Eddie was high up in the prize-money lists as a losing semi-finalist, 6–5, against Cliff Thorburn, and again, as a losing quarter-finalist to Steve Davis in the 1983 World Professional Championship. Having reached the semi-finals of the 1983 Jameson International, Eddie suffered another defeat by a very much in-form Steve Davis and won only two frames to Davis's nine.

Eddie remained in the UK to pick up some very useful minor prizes in other big tournaments, including the 1984 Lada Classic (quarter-finalist), the Benson and Hedges and the Yamaha International Masters. After the 1984 World Championship, where he lost to Jimmy White in the second round, Eddie's current position in the World Ranking List is sixth.

Fred Davis

One of the most famous names of the Snooker world, Fred Davis was born at Whittingham Moor, near Chesterfield, the younger brother of the legendary Joe Davis by some twelve years. He became Boys Billiards Champion at fifteen and, following his brother's example, gradually turned to the more popular game of snooker.

In 1940 Fred met brother Joe for the World title and lost by only one frame, 37–36. His first World Championship title was gained in 1948 against the late Walter Donaldson. Since then Fred has won the World Championship on nine occasions, including the officially unrecognised game against George Chenier of Canada in 1958. One of his proudest achievements was his defeat of his brother in the *Empire News* tournament in 1948. He was also the holder of the UK Professional Billiards title, which he won by beating Kingsley Kennerley in 1951.

He played in all the *Pot Black* series from 1969 to 1973, and won the Highest Break prize in 1970 and 1971. Ill-health prevented Fred from appearing in the 1974 *Pot Black* competition and he was ordered by his doctor to take a complete rest.

He returned to compete in the World Championships at Belle Vue, Manchester, in April 1974. Although lacking in match practice, Fred, now sixty-two, played superbly. His victory over the Canadian Champion, Bill Werbeniuk, took him into the quarter-finals to face the formidable Alex Higgins. Davis won by 15 frames to 14 but the following day this struggle had obviously affected Fred's stamina and he failed against Reardon in the semi-finals.

Fred was once again a member of the 1975 *Pot Black* 'squad', winning the Highest Break prize with a score of 87. His cheque was presented to him after the final frame by his brother Joe.

Fred started the 1976 *Pot Black* series off well by beating Willie Thorne, some forty years his junior, by 88 points to 28. However, he lost against Rex Williams and Dennis Taylor in later rounds. In the World Championships at Manchester he battled bravely against Eddie Charlton in the quarter-finals to lose by just two frames.

He failed to reach the quarter-finals of the 1977 World Championship at Sheffield, being beaten in the first round by his old rival John Pulman. However, later that year Fred was to have the consolation of being awarded the OBE for services to snooker. This makes a unique snooker 'double' as his brother Joe had also been awarded the OBE some years earlier.

Back in the Championship for the 1978 World title Fred was in excellent form and, wearing contact lenses instead

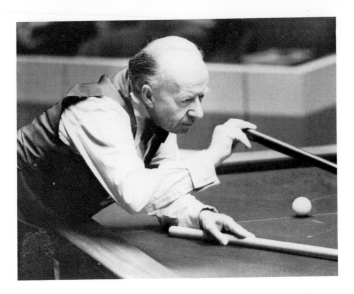

of his famous 'swivel-lens' spectacles, he defeated two much younger players, Dennis Taylor and the UK Professional Champion Patsy Fagan. This took him into the semi-finals but, in spite of a tremendous display of his old skills, his opponent from South Africa, Perrie Mans, finally won the game by 18 frames to 16.

Fred was, once again, among the eight players in *Pot Black* 1979, where he played – and lost to – the young Steve Davis and Perrie Mans. His only victory, over the defending Champion, Doug Mountjoy, was not enough to see him through to the semi-finals. He was defeated by Eddie Charlton in the 1979 World Championship quarter-finals after winning his first-round match against the Canadian Kirk Stevens.

Another disappointment for Fred in early 1979 came when he unsuccessfully defended his twenty-eight-year-old title of UK Professional Billiards Champion. He lost his semi-final game to another name of the past, John Barrie, by 1548 points to 1031. However, Fred did reach the Final of the Castle Open competition at the Castle Club, Southampton, beating Willie Thorne and Cliff Thorburn. Although, at the age of sixty-five, he lost to Alex Higgins in the Final, he shared the enthusiastic applause given to both players at the end of the game.

Throughout the remainder of 1979 and on into 1980,

Fred continued to compete at both billiards and snooker. He played for England, with John Spencer and Graham Miles, in the State Express World Cup, making breaks of 55 and 63. His other engagements included the Coral UK at Preston, the Padmore/Super Crystalate International, the Benson and Hedges Masters, the British Gold Cup, the Pontin's Festival and, of course, the World Championship at Sheffield. At the age of sixty-six he realised a lifelong ambition when, in May 1980, he won the Yorkshire Bank-sponsored World Professional Billiards Championship in a challenge match against the holder, Rex Williams. Played over four days at the Northern Snooker Centre in Leeds, the final scores were: Davis 5978 points, Williams 4452. Fred now joins his late brother Joe as the only players to have won both the World Billiards and World Snooker Championships.

In November 1980, Fred successfully defended his World Billiards Champion title at the Brownsover Hall Hotel in Rugby. Among his opponents were Rex Williams, Jack Karnehm, Kingsley Kennerley and Steve Davis. The beaten finalist, however, was Mark Wildman of Peterborough who had been playing professionally for only twelve months. The UK Professional Billiards Championship, at the Winter Gardens, Margate, in February 1981 resulted in a semi-final defeat for Fred by his old rival, Rex Williams.

After a disappointing performance in the 1981 World Championship, Fred threatened to retire altogether from championship play. However, and not too surprisingly, he changed his mind and, after losing to Rex Williams in the semi-finals of the World Billiards Championship, Fred was once again at Sheffield for the World Snooker Championship. Seeded 12, the oldest player lost to the youngest player, Dean Reynolds, the 1981 *Junior Pot Black* Champion, by 10 frames to 7 in the first round. Fred battled bravely in the 1983 UK Professional Billiards Championship, reaching the Final where he lost to Mark Wildman. He put up a similar performance in the World Professional Billiards Championship succumbing only to Rex Williams in the Final. He lost again, incidentally, to Rex in the qualifying round of the 1983 World Professional Snooker Championship.

In 1984, Fred lost to Eddie Charlton in the semi-finals of the World Billiards Championship, played at the Majestic

Snooker Club, Portsmouth, and to Bill Werbeniuk, 10–4, in the first round of the World Championship at Sheffield. Fred and his family moved a short while ago from their farm in Worcestershire to a new home in North Wales. Snooker's 'senior citizen' celebrated his seventy-first birthday in August 1984.

ESSENTIALS OF GOOD POTTING
by Fred Davis

It seems to me that some people have a good, straight steady cue-action from the first moment they start to play. Within a few games they are banging down all the so-called easy ones without any trouble, and they get ahead with the rest of the game much quicker than others because they do not have to worry overmuch about whether the ball is going down or not. Others have potting troubles all their lives – even men who are good at the other departments of the game, players whose strength is good, who have an uncanny knowledge of the angles and who can lay a deadly snooker. It is almost pitiful to see them make a lovely positional shot and then fail to knock the colour in.

One of the reasons is a badly made bridge; another is a habit of moving some part of the body on the stroke. But there are players who conform in these respects and still cannot rely on their potting. They tell you that one day it seems easy, and the next even the simple ones are difficult. These players suffer from cue wobble. I should think the percentage is very high indeed, and the odd thing is that players who have been at the game for twenty years and play reasonably well on a club standard still suffer from it.

This is the complaint which I think you may never have or you may always have – unless you know how it is caused. It depends at the outset of your playing career on how you pick up and hold your cue. This, in turn, depends on the length of your cue, and its balance. Much of the trouble of side-to-side wobble is caused by having the cue-hold too far back. Ideally, the book tells us, the forearm, at rest, should drop perpendicularly from the elbow and the grip should be about one inch from the end of the butt. But it is ridiculous to lay down such rules. Cues in any club rack vary in length up to nine inches, and

49

in weight as much as three ounces. Arm-lengths vary.

I believe in a short, sturdy cue, not because I am a short man but because I believe a short cue is better for snooker than a long one. Short back action means greater accuracy in the drive. I also believe in the cue-hold being slightly *in front* of the vertical, but I see many, many players whose grip is *behind* the vertical. When I point it out, they are surprised; they didn't know. I like to get as close to the shot as possible, because I find that the closer I get the more control I have over what I am doing. The long sawing movements with long cues, with flowing finishes, are not for this game. Snooker requires compactness.

I believe in a short back swing and a good follow-through, but even the follow-through must be strictly controlled, and the cue held rigidly on the line. A good follow-through doesn't mean a flowing, meandering action. I like to be well forward over the left knee to get into the shot, but this may not suit you – it depends on your height.

Another important point is to keep the cue running close to the body – that is, brushing against the waistcoat without being buried in it. All these factors make for compactness – elbow well up, hand slightly in advance of elbow, good solid grip on the cue, hand wrapped well round the cue, and no pencil grip: these build up to a short, level, reasonably wobble-proof cue movement. If you have any wobble at all you must rid yourself of it, and at once you will know the joys of really good potting.

Maybe I should mention one further point. Many have cue wobble because they stand facing the shot too squarely. Stand at an angle of forty-five degrees. The turning of the trunk to face the line of the shot causes some necessary tightness and tension, which all helps to fix the stance firmly.

FRED DAVIS ON SNOOKER

Middle-aged snooker players are the Micawbers of the sporting world. They are always hoping that something will happen to their style of play which will make them a black or two better. Like golfers they never give up hope, and why should they?

I have, in fact, helped a number of men aged over fifty to

play better, and there are some who will say they are playing better now than they did twenty years ago. This is because I was able to point out faults in their stance or action which they had never been aware of. Quite small alterations to stance, for instance, will immediately make a player feel more comfortable and enable him to keep his cue on the line.

It has yet to be proved that age really matters at all in snooker, beyond the pure fatigue of standing up for a dozen stiff frames a day in championship stuff. I know that some whose snooker is not what it was can be heard to plead that their eyesight is not so good. To me, that is nonsense. I couldn't see so well in my early twenties, but I had an adjustment made to my spectacle frames and have worn glasses ever since. Plenty of top-class players wear glasses, and if youth is scoring well in the amateur championships, that is rather because the great players who are over fifty are mostly billiards players who have never concentrated on snooker to the same degree as the youngsters.

Still, to the hard-working office type, whose brain is active five days a week, and whose digestion perhaps is not what it was, some falling off is likely. What is to be done? First, I suggest, is to recognise that your eyesight is not to blame – or if it is, to do something about it. Second, you may find that the main trouble is deterioration of your power of co-ordination. In short, the timing is no longer so sweet. You tend to hurry to get the actual shot over, or you come up on the stroke. The faults which you always made are now worse, too. The trivial things, such as too tight a grip, or a sloppy bridge, or that all-too-flowing swing, are exaggerated. You worry about your failures.

Well, I don't get any younger either. So I can prescribe with first-hand knowledge of the disease of gradual ageing. My prescription is twofold. Chiefly, you must learn to play within your powers. Don't play when you are tired. Don't play too many frames without a rest. And when you rest, even while your opponent is in a break, relax! Don't play as if life itself depended on winning; for that creates tension, which is fatal to timing.

Try to discover for yourself a more leisurely technique. By this I mean that, without being careless, you should move casually to your stroke, avoid the shots you are quite sure you won't bring off, play for snookers when you know that for you that is better than the bravado type of attempt at potting, and generally use your head like the cunning old fox.

The second piece of advice is to get a good player to play a frame with you and tell you afterwards, quite frankly, why you are missing them. Often you'll be astonished at the advice he will give you. He will see things, and may tell you things he has known about your play for years. It's a curious thing that although in golf anyone will offer you advice gratis and unasked, in snooker no one ever tells you unless you ask. Best of all, of course, is to have a couple of sessions with a professional. Any ordinary player, and I don't care how bad or how old he is, will benefit from a lesson from a pro, and do so practically at once.

There is also this matter of getting the chin down to the cue. Perhaps, owing to your maturing build, you now find this very difficult. If so, don't try. That great little Canadian George Chenier, who was here some years ago, played with a semi-upright stance, almost like the style of old John Roberts, yet he made a break which was then the world's record, of 144. True he afterwards adopted the English style, but I doubt if he played better as a result. He proved that it isn't necessary to get the chin down to the level of the cue to play brilliant snooker. So why should you force yourself into a position which is a strain?

If you are in your fifties, you have plenty of good snooker in you yet, if you take it easy.

Steve Davis

In 1957, the year that Steve was born in Plumstead, London, the World Snooker Championship Trophy was still in the possession of the famous Davis brothers, Joe and Fred. As Steve Davis (no relation) said in 1980, 'When I was a kid, I dreamed of playing in the World Championship – it's probably every youngster's ambition.' Just twelve months later Steve not only realised that ambition for the second time, but had his own name inscribed upon that coveted cup as the 1981 World Champion.

Steve began playing snooker at the age of fifteen at a holiday camp. Coached mainly by his father, Steve won

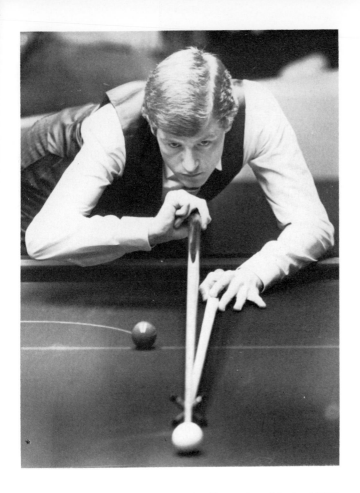

the All England Junior Billiards Championship in 1976, reaching the semi-finals of the corresponding snooker competition. In August 1977 he made the elusive break of 147, won the Lucania Pro-Am and National Championship and, for good measure, the London and Home Counties Silver Jubilee Tournament. He was then selected to play for the English International team in April 1978 and went on to win the Pontin's Open Championship, defeating Ray Reardon and Dennis Taylor.

Steve's next victory was in the CIU Snooker Tournament, and in one of his last matches as an amateur he retained his Lucania Pro-Am title with a comfortable win over Patsy Fagan. Playing for the first time in the Canadian Open Tournament, Steve defeated Willie Thorne 9–3 but lost to Alex Higgins in the quarter-finals. His application for professional status was accepted on 17 September 1978.

In December of that year Steve made his television début in *Pot Black*. His first opponent, fittingly enough, was Fred Davis – over forty years older in both age and experience. Showing no signs of being overawed by his illustrious adversary, Steve scored a convincing victory by 83 points to 23. The tables (or table) were turned against him in his next game when Doug Mountjoy won by 97 points to 26, and Steve's chances of staying in the competition faded when he lost to Perrie Mans 60–45.

1979 was also the first year that Steve qualified to enter the World Championship. He survived to the first round by beating Ian Anderson (Australia) and Patsy Fagan (Ireland). Steve played well against the eventual finalist, Dennis Taylor, losing the 25-frame match by only 13–11. His next big engagement was the Pontin's Snooker Festival and, unlike 1978 when he received 30 points start from the established players, this time he, too, had to give 30 points start to his amateur opponents. There were 1034 entries and at the end of the mammoth tournament the winner was – Steve Davis, who beat the up-and-coming English Amateur Champion Jimmy White in the Final.

Steve later toured throughout Great Britain in a challenge series against Fred Davis, playing at some twelve clubs and travelling several thousand miles. The last game was held at Steve's home club at Romford where he was the winner by 9–3. It was here, too, that Steve played Alex Higgins in a marathon best of 65 frames challenge match and beat the Irish Champion 33–23. Steve met Jimmy White again in the Canadian 'Open' in the autumn of 1979, scoring a convincing 9–3 victory in the seventh round, but in his next game – the quarter-finals – the opposition came from the Canadian Champion, Cliff Thorburn. Despite breaks of 92, 100 and 120, the Londoner lost by 9 frames to 6.

One of Steve's best performances in his young career was achieved during the 1980 World Championship. After having beaten Patsy Fagan in the first round, he knocked out Terry Griffiths, the reigning Champion, in the second round by 13 frames to 10! It looked as if his manager's prophecy was about to come true, but his opponent in the quarter-finals was Alex Higgins. Although losing by 13 frames to 9 it was during this match that Steve cleared the table with a break of 136, sharing the £1000 prize for the highest break in the tournament with the Canadian Kirk Stevens. At the Pontin's Festival at Prestatyn, shortly after the World Championship, Steve again beat Terry Griffiths but he played disappointingly against John Virgo in the semi-finals, losing by 5 frames to 3. Revenge, however, came swiftly. Just a few days later, and at another holiday camp, Warner's on Hayling Island, Steve won the £2000 first prize in the GAME 'Open' Tournament, beating Virgo by 4 frames to nil in the semi-finals on the way.

Steve's progress was now in the ascendant and in November 1980 he won the Coral United Kingdom Championship with a 16 frames to 6 victory over Alex Higgins. Four days later he took the Wilson's Classic against Dennis Taylor. One of his less successful competitions was in *Pot Black* 81, where he failed to reach the semi-finals. However, Steve hit the sporting headlines again when he won the first prize of £10,000 in the Yamaha Organs Trophy at Derby in March 1981, beating David Taylor 9–6 in the Final, and another £4000 in the John Courage English Professional Championship.

As the No. 13 seed, Steve then entered the World Championship at Sheffield for the second time. His success is now part of snooker history, but a reminder of the opponents he defeated – Jimmy White, Alex Higgins, Terry Griffiths, Cliff Thorburn and Doug Mountjoy – serves to illustrate just what a hard-fought and well-deserved victory he achieved.

The next twelve months were to be, perhaps, the most eventful in any snooker player's career in the game's history. Steve rapidly earned the reputation of being unbeatable – which he was – at least in the major tournaments for several months. His list of lucrative victories included the Jameson International, beating Dennis Taylor 9–0 in the Final, the State Express World Team Classic (as England's captain), the Coral UK, beating Terry Griffiths by 16 frames to 3, the Benson and Hedges Masters, again beating Terry Griffiths, the Yamaha Organs Trophy, the Tolly Cobbold Classic and, for good measure, the 1982 *Pot Black* Championship! True, Steve finished as runner-up in the Lada Classic to Griffiths, 9–8, but achieved the first televised 147 break, against John Spencer in the quarter-finals. He also lost to Griffiths, 5–9, in the Benson and Hedges Irish Masters, and to Jimmy White, 9–11, in the Northern Ireland Classic. Possibly no result since he won the 1981 World Championship was as sensational as Steve's defeat, 10–1, by the 150-1 outsider, Tony Knowles, in the first round of the 1982 event. Davis was unable to explain this débâcle, but later admitted that Knowles had played well and 'he never made any mistakes to let me in'.

The next twelve months, however, saw a 'new improved' Steve Davis as he put together a long string of successes. They included the Pontin's professional tournament, the Lang's Supreme Scottish Masters, the Hofmeister World Doubles (with Tony Meo), the Lada Classic, the Tolly Cobbold Classic, the Benson and Hedges Irish Masters, and the 1983 *Pot Black* Championship. Steve's ultimate achievement was once again at the Crucible Theatre, Sheffield, in May where he scored an overwhelming victory over Cliff Thorburn, 18–6, to regain the World Championship title.

Steve began the 1983–4 season where he had left off, scotching Tony Knowles' hopes in the Final of the Lang's Supreme Masters by 9 frames to 6, to win the event for the second year in succession. The Final of the 1983 Jameson International, held at the Eldon Square Recreation Centre, Newcastle, was another confrontation between Steve and Cliff Thorburn, with Steve once again proving himself unbeatable, winning by 9 frames to 4 and adding £24,000 to his bank account. Yet another profitable result followed when he led the England team to victory over Wales in the State Express Team Classic at Reading.

Steve continued to maintain his almost unbeatable record throughout the season, winning the Hofmeister World Doubles Championship (with Tony Meo), the Lada Classic again (against Tony Meo!), the Yamaha International Masters, the Tolly Cobbold Classic, the Benson and Hedges Irish Masters and for the third time the World Championship, 18–16, against fellow Londoner Jimmy White. His most notable defeat occurred in the Coral UK where Alex Higgins rallied from a 7 frames to nil deficit to win by 16 frames to 15. Strangely, Steve also failed to defend his *Pot Black* title in 1984, losing his 'knock-out' quarter-final frame to Jimmy White. Nevertheless, Steve still heads the World Ranking List in the coveted No.1 position.

Ray Edmonds

A successful amateur for nearly two decades, Ray's name first appeared in the record books as the runner-up in the 1961 England Amateur Championship. He comes from Lincolnshire and was for many years his county's Snooker and Billiards Champion. He is now the manager of a painting and decorating company in Grimsby. Ray was beaten in the Northern Section Final of the 1963 England Amateur Championship by Gary Owen and continued to be unsuccessful in this event until he won it in 1969 by 11 frames to 9 against Jonathan Barron. He was to be twice runner-up again in 1972 and 1973. At Cardiff in 1972, Ray defeated Jonathan Barron once more in the semi-finals of the World Amateur Championship, going on to win in the final against the South African player Mannie Francisco by 11 frames to 10. Two years later in Dublin he retained his World Amateur title against Geoff Thomas (Wales) but, going for the hat-trick in Johannesburg in 1976, he lost in the quarter-finals.

Ray has been a professional since 1978 and his results

in the World Championships to date are: 1979, lost to Roy Andrewartha, 9–8; 1980, lost to Dennis Taylor in the first round, 10–3; 1981, lost to John Spencer in the first round, 10–9. He was a semi-finalist in the 1981 John Courage English Professional Championship, losing to Steve Davis, 9–0. Ray's accomplished billiards playing, however, brought him two major victories in 1981 – the Guinness 'Open' on the Isle of Wight and the Midas 'Masters' at Margate.

In the 1982 Yamaha International Masters Ray reached the Group A semi-finals, winning against Dennis Taylor but losing to Steve Davis and John Virgo. He made another attempt at the World Billiards title in March at La Reserve, Sutton Coldfield, but again lost in the semi-finals, to Mark Wildman of Peterborough. Then his qualifying match for the 1982 World Snooker Championship (also at La Reserve) resulted in a 9–6 defeat by the 1981 *Junior Pot Black* Champion Dean Reynolds. Fate and the draw brought the same two players together again in the qualifying round for the 1983 World Championship. The result also was the same – Ray losing to Dean by 10 frames to 6. Ray made little impact in the 1983 Jameson International, the 1984 Coral UK, Lada Classic or the Yamaha International Masters. He failed to reach the first round of the 1984 World Championship losing 10–9 to the South African Jimmy van Rensburg in a qualifier. Turning to billiards, Ray was a losing semi-finalist in both the 1983 UK Professional and World Professional Championships. He is now heard regularly as a TV snooker commentator and is the proud manager of his own snooker centre in Grimsby.

Patsy Fagan

As an amateur Patsy Fagan – a Dubliner by birth but a Londoner by adoption – reached the Final of the English Championship against Ray Edmonds in 1974, losing by 11 frames to 7. He represented Ireland in the 1975–6 Home Internationals, winning two of his three matches including one against Willie Thorne. He was again the losing finalist for the Southern Championship in 1976 but scored a record break of 115 during the competition.

Fagan turned professional in 1976 and went on to

defeat Jim Meadowcroft in the qualifying rounds of the 1977 World Championship before losing to Ray Reardon by 13 frames to 7 in the next round. The Irishman's reputation was really established in 1978 with victories over John Virgo and Doug Mountjoy to win the title of UK Professional Champion in the contest sponsored by Super Crystalate. This was followed by another success in the Dry Blackthorn Cup at Wembley, when Fagan beat John Spencer and then Alex Higgins in the Final.

In the 1978 World Championship Patsy defeated Higgins yet again to reach the quarter-finals. He took the last frame from Alex in a dramatic finish after both players had won 12 frames each. Unfortunately for Fagan, he met veteran Fred Davis in his old form in the next session and was forced to exit from the Championship gracefully with the score at Davis 13, Fagan 10.

Subsequent tournaments have not proved too encouraging for the Irish player's record book and he is still trying to recapture his earlier winning form. In the *Daily*

Mirror's 'Champion of Champions' he was beaten 6–1 by Ray Reardon in the semi-finals, and John Spencer also beat him during the first round of the Holsten Lager International. Patsy's 1978 UK Professional title was defended unsuccessfully at the Guildhall, Preston, when he lost to David Taylor, 9–7, in the first round. He fared no better in the 1979 World Championship, with a 9–3 defeat in a preliminary round by the young Londoner Steve Davis. He was a member of the 'Rest Of The World' team in the State Express World Challenge Cup, but neither he nor his two companions, Perrie Mans and Jimmy van Rensburg of South Africa, could make much impression on their opponents from England and Northern Ireland. Patsy did put up a better performance in the Coral UK Championship, beating Pat Hallet of Grimsby and Graham Miles before succumbing to Dennis Taylor in the quarter-finals. In the 1980 World Championship it was a case of history repeating itself when his chance of surviving the first round was destroyed once again by Steve Davis, who won by 10 frames to 6.

Patsy played again for Ireland in the 1980 State Express World Cup. Despite some individual victories, his team lost to Wales in the semi-finals. In the second round of the Coral UK Championship, Fagan, the 1977 winner, produced some of his best form to lose by one frame, 9–8, to Terry Griffiths, but the 1981 World Championship was, once again, unlucky when he failed to win his qualifying-round match, 9–7, against John Dunning.

Since then less than moderate success has followed Patsy. He lost to Alex Higgins, 5–3, in the second round of the 1982 Jameson International at Stockport, and in the Coral UK he exited in the first round against Mike Hallett of Grimsby. His form improved in the 1982 World Championship, albeit briefly, by beating David Taylor, 10–9, in the first round before he suffered another second-round defeat, 13–7, against the Canadian Kirk Stevens. In the 1982 Irish Professional Championship Patsy lost his second-round match against Tommy Murphy, 6–2. In the qualifying groups for the 1983 Jameson International he was beaten 5–1 by the Snooka-sport promoter Mike Watterson, but reached the second round of the Coral UK before losing to Steve Davis, 9–3. He was a losing semi-finalist (to Dennis Taylor) in the Irish Professional Championship at the Maysfield Leisure

Centre, Belfast, and sank without trace in the early stages of both the Yamaha International and the 1983 World Championship. Patsy had another lean year up until the 1984 World Championship, being well out of the major prize-money in the Professional Players Tournament, the Hofmeister World Doubles, the Lada Classic and also the Yamaha International. His qualifying game against Jim Wych in the World Championship ended in a 10–3 defeat.

Neal Foulds

Born in 1963, at Perivale, Middlesex, Neal inherited the love of the game from his father, Geoff, then a very talented amateur – both are now professionals! Neal began playing at around the age of eleven, coached by his father, and after leaving school took up the game full-time at the Neasden Snooker Club where he was further encouraged by former England Amateur Champion Ron Gross. Brief highlights of Neal's career to date: London and Home Counties Junior Champion 1979; runner-up in the 'World' Junior Championship; television début in *Junior Pot Black* 1981; British Junior Under 19 Champion 1982; Warner's 'Open' winner in 1983; turned professional June 1983; partnered his father in the Hofmeister World Doubles.

In the 1984 World Championship Neal realised every young – and not so young – player's dream by defeating Alex Higgins 10–9 in the first round. Although he lost 13–6 to Doug Mountjoy in the second round, Neal has rapidly established himself as one of today's most promising young professionals. By reaching the last sixteen in the 1984 World Championship, he also qualifies for inclusion in the 1985 *Pot Black* series.

Silvino Francisco

The dark-featured and skilful South African player made his UK and television début in the 1982 World Championship, where he created one of the first-round surprise results in defeating the No. 5 seed, Dennis Taylor. He then beat *Junior Pot Black* Champion Dean Reynolds, to reach the quarter-finals but found that he was unable to overcome the former World Champion Ray Reardon, losing by 13 frames to 8.

Silvino was born in Cape Town in May 1946 of Portuguese descent. He was the South Africa Snooker Champion in 1968 and Billiards Champion in 1972. He won both titles on further occasions, emulating the achievements of his older and better-known brother, Manuel. For the remainder of the 1982 season Silvino remained in England for club and summer engagements.

Silvino became based at Chesterfield, but the general public saw little of him until he re-emerged as the seventeenth seed for the 1983 World Championship at Sheffield. Ironically enough, his opponent in the first round was yet again Dennis Taylor, and this time the Irishman was the victor by 10 frames to 9. Silvino – who has a son of the same name – competed later in the Pontin's Professional at Brean Sands, defeating John Virgo 5–0 in the semi-finals, but losing 9–7 to Tony Meo in the Final. In the Pairs event, where he was partnered by Cliff Wilson, Silvino was a losing semi-finalist to John Spencer and John Virgo. He reached the quarter-final stages in the 1983 Jameson International but was unable, like everyone else, to overcome Steve Davis in that important tournament. His career in the UK has now included his first appearance in *Pot Black*, reaching the quarter-finals of the 1984 series. He lost 5–1 to Mark

Wildman in the first round of the Lada Classic but later showed better form in the 1984 World Championship, reaching the second round by beating Tony Meo 10–5 before losing 13–8 to Ray Reardon. Beaten by Jimmy van Rensberg in the semi-finals of the 1984 South African Open, Silvino is ranked number 17 in the 1984 list. Silvino has made over 300 century breaks, including a 147. He is a South African Billiards Champion and a Masters Champion. His hobbies are diving, squash and fishing.

Terry Griffiths

Until the BBC Television and press coverage of the 1979 World Championship from Sheffield, relatively few snooker enthusiasts were familiar with the name of Terry Griffiths. He was born and still lives in Llanelli where he had a variety of jobs, including that of postman. Terry, born in 1947, started playing snooker around the age of fifteen in his local billiard halls. 'I started when I was young, but I never had any coaching. I watched and listened to other players.'

A natural ability at the game turned into a talent that entitled him to enter the Welsh Amateur Championships. He was the losing finalist in 1972 and was subsequently selected to represent Wales in Home International matches. Terry won most of his games in these events between 1973 and 1976. Meanwhile, in 1975, he did, at last, win the Welsh Amateur Championship. In November 1976 he reached the quarter-finals of the World Amateur Championship in Johannesburg but lost to the South African player Jimmy van Rensburg 5–3. Terry's next success was in the spring of 1977, winning the English Amateur Championship and overwhelming Sid Hood of Grimsby 13–3. In the spring of 1978 he won the title for the second time, against Joe Johnson of Bradford, 13–5. Shortly afterwards his application to turn professional was accepted.

Terry provided the snooker sensation of 1979 when he won the World Snooker Championship at his first attempt. Later in the year two narrow defeats prevented him from adding two more important titles to his crown: in the Final of the Canadian 'Open', at Toronto, he lost by 17–16 to Cliff Thorburn; and again by 14–13 to John Virgo in the Final of the Coral UK Championship at Preston. He was invited to compete in *Pot Black* 80 but did not reach the semi-finals, losing two games out of three. His major success in becoming World Champion, however, was recognised in January 1980 when Terry was the 'victim' of *This is Your Life*.

A few weeks later Terry was back in form when he beat Cliff Thorburn, John Spencer and Alex Higgins to win the Benson and Hedges Masters at the Wembley Conference Centre. His bid to become World Champion for the second year running, however, was foiled by the young London professional Steve Davis when they met in the second round at Sheffield's Crucible Theatre. Losing by 13 frames to 10 the Welshman would have to wait twelve months to have another chance of retrieving his title. Nevertheless, Terry swallowed his disappointment and spent the rest of the competition adding his comments on the play from the vantage point of a seat in the BBC TV commentary box.

Terry enjoyed mixed fortunes during the following twelve months. In September he lost to Cliff Thorburn, 17–10, in the Final of the Canadian Open. He was one of the winning Welsh team for the State Express World Cup, played at the New London Theatre. A heavy defeat in the Coral UK Championship semi-finals, 9–0, by Steve Davis followed in November, and he lost to Alex Higgins in the Benson and Hedges Masters Final, 9–6, in January and to Ray Reardon, also 9–6, in the semi-finals of the Woodpecker Welsh Professional Championship in February. But that month Terry retained his title in the Benson and Hedges Irish Masters tournament with a prize of £5000 after defeating Ray Reardon, 9–7. The 1981 World Championship, unhappily for the 1979 Champion, brought him against Steve Davis for the second year running and once again Terry lost to the Londoner, by 13 frames to 9 in the quarter-finals. In the Pontin's Professional tournament, shortly after, Terry beat Steve 5–2 in the first round, going on to win the competition, 9–8. against Willie Thorne.

September 1982 saw Terry beaten by Alex Higgins, 5–2, in the quarter-finals of the Jameson International, and winning a minor event against Fred Davis at the Sheffield Snooker Centre. In October the Welsh team of Griffiths, Mountjoy and Reardon were the beaten finalists in the State Express World Team Classic. Terry's next important tournament was the Coral UK at the Guildhall, Preston. Losing to Steve Davis in the Final, Terry nevertheless picked up the useful runner-up prize of £5000, plus £1000 as the scorer of the highest break – 131 against Tony Knowles. Steve Davis and Terry were again the finalists in the Lada Classic at Oldham, with Terry winning narrowly 9–8, and their next big clash was in the Final of the Benson and Hedges Masters. This time it was Steve's turn to win, by 9 frames to 5. Their saga continued in the Yamaha Organs Trophy, Steve winning 9–7 in the Final, and in the Benson and Hedges Irish Masters, where Terry triumphed over Steve, 9–5. When Steve Davis departed in the first round of the 1982 World Championship, Terry became the automatic favourite to take the title for the second time, yet a similar fate awaited the No. 3 seed when he was beaten, 10–6, by Willie Thorne – another first-round shock result!

Despite this unwelcome blow to his fortunes, Terry maintained his cool and dedicated approach to the game, and before long it paid fresh dividends. Within the next few months he came to the fore again by winning the Coral UK Championship from Alex Higgins, 16–15. Then, in an otherwise moderate but lucrative season, Terry was the runner-up to Steve Davis in the Tolly Cobbold Classic and, with Doug Mountjoy, to Steve Davis and Tony Meo in the World Doubles Final. He scored the highest breaks in the World Team Classic (123) and in the Benson and Hedges Masters (128). The former World Champion made his fifth attempt at the title in 1983 as the fourteenth seed, but only reached the second round, losing narrowly, 13–12, to Cliff Thorburn. But once again Terry proved what a formidable opponent he can be when, in the summer of 1983, he won the Pontin's Open at Prestatyn (where there were 945 entries) against Ray Reardon in the Final.

In 1984 Terry maintained his high standard of play and proved continually to be a dangerous opponent in nearly every major competition. His most successful tournaments were the Jameson International, in which he was a semi-finalist, the State Express World Team Classic, as captain of the Welsh runners-up to England, the Benson and Hedges Masters, in which he was beaten 9–5 by Jimmy White in the Final and, at the second attempt, the 1984 *Pot Black* Championship, which he won against John Spencer. His bid to win the World Championship for the second time got him as far as the quarter-finals and he battled bravely before succumbing to Steve Davis, his stable-mate, by 13 frames to 10. Terry's second book, *Complete Snooker*, was published in the spring of 1984. He is number eight in the World Ranking List.

Alex Higgins

Alex learnt to play snooker in a Belfast billiard hall called The Jampot after being invited for a game by friends. He was ten years old. 'Within a few weeks I was making breaks of twenty and thirty and had left most of the lads behind. I was completely self-taught, but I soon got the feel of a cue and it was not long before I realised I had great natural ability.'

He won the Irish amateur title and after moving to Lancashire he entered the 1972 World Professional Championship. On his way to the Final against John Spencer, Alex, by now called 'Hurricane' Higgins, had to play in the qualifying rounds and defeated Ron Gross and Jack Rea. Into the quarter-finals, he beat John Pulman 31–23 and won by the odd frame in the semi-finals against Rex Williams, 31–30. His victory over Spencer in Birmingham was achieved by 37 frames to 32 and Higgins, at the age of twenty-two, became the youngest title-holder in snooker history.

Higgins was invited to play in the 1973 *Pot Black* series and obliged his followers in the first programme with a break of 60, beating John Pulman 101–50. However, the title of *Pot Black* Champion eluded him and he was beaten by Rex Williams, Jack Rea and Fred Davis.

On his way to the Final of the 1976 World Championship Alex had narrowly defeated Cliff Thorburn, John

Spencer and Eddie Charlton. In the 53-frame Final, however, Ray Reardon was at his best, winning 27–16. Revenge for Higgins came at Leeds shortly after when he beat Reardon for the £1000 first prize in the Canadian Club Tournament.

Alex was knocked out in the first round of the 1977 World Championship by Doug Mountjoy, the 1978 *Pot Black* Champion. The winning margin was a solitary frame, 13–12, and the match was decided on the last black of the 25th frame. History repeated itself, unluckily for Alex, when in the 1978 World Championship he played and lost against Patsy Fagan with the scores again at 13–12. Alex, who had defeated Dennis Taylor to retain his Irish Professional title, successfully met another challenge, from Dubliner Patsy Fagan, in 1978. The game was held at the Ulster Hall, Belfast, with Higgins winning by 21 frames to 13. He also won the 1977 Canadian Open Championship, beating John Spencer by 17 to 14 at the National Exhibition Centre at Toronto. Playing in the 1978 *Pot Black* series, his second appearance, Alex lost to Dennis Taylor and Doug Mountjoy. His one victory, over Ray Reardon by 90 to 53, included a 50 break which took Alex just three minutes!

One of his best triumphs in 1978 came in the Benson and Hedges Masters at the New London Theatre, Drury Lane. He won 4–3 in the quarter-finals against Dennis Taylor, and then heavily defeated Ray Reardon 5–1 in the semi-finals. The other finalist, Cliff Thorburn, had previously beaten Doug Mountjoy and John Spencer. The result was a victory for Alex 7–5, and a cheque for £3000. He surprisingly lost to David Taylor in the semi-finals of the UK Professional Championship later in the year, and also to the young Tony Meo in the semi-finals of the Canadian Open Championship at Toronto.

Early in 1979 Alex experienced yet another semi-final defeat, this time by Graham Miles in the Holsten Lager Tournament. His game against Terry Griffiths in the 1979 World Championship was one of the highlights of the entire tournament. Their quarter-final encounter resulted in a win for Griffiths in the final frame with the scores level at 12 frames each! As one of the UK challengers for the 1979 Canadian International at Toronto, having beaten two other Canadians, Alex played Cliff Thorburn in the semi-finals but lost 9–6.

1980 was a busy year for Alex with some 'hits' and very near misses. He lost his Irish Professional title to Dennis Taylor in a match played at the Ulster Hall, Belfast, by 21 frames to 15, and was runner-up to John Spencer in the Wilson's Classic and to Terry Griffiths in the Benson and Hedges Masters. His major successes, however, came in the Tolly Cobbold, the Padmore/Super Crystalate International (against Perrie Mans), and the British Gold Cup, in which he beat Ray Reardon in the Final. He got to within two frames of becoming the World Champion for the second time when he lost to Cliff Thorburn in the 1980 Final by 18 frames to 16.

Enjoying the somewhat more relaxed atmosphere of Pontin's holiday village at Camber Sands a few days later, Alex won the professional competition, beating Dennis Taylor 9–7. At Toronto in September he lost to Terry Griffiths in the semi-finals of the Canadian Open, and failed by 16 frames to 6 against Steve Davis in the Final of the Coral UK at Preston Guildhall in November. He played in *Pot Black* 81 but only took one frame out of three in the qualifying round.

The Irishman's winning streak returned in January 1981 at the Wembley Conference Hall with the £6000 first prize in the Benson and Hedges Masters, beating Cliff

Thorburn in the semi-finals and Terry Griffiths in the Final. Oddly enough, in the Benson and Hedges Irish Masters Alex lost in the semi-finals to Welshman Ray Reardon! In January 1981 the 'Hurricane' became the third snooker professional to be 'subject' on *This is Your Life*, but his appearance in the World Snooker Championship, where he was seeded fourth, was limited to one round in which he lost to Steve Davis, 13–8. He later blamed too busy an engagement diary prior to the tournament for his loss of form and 'sparkle'.

Although Alex lost two 'good conduct' marks after the 1981 World Championship, dropping to eleventh place in the world ratings, he returned in triumph to the 1982 event at the Crucible Theatre, Sheffield. Playing his best snooker for nearly a decade, Alex defeated a formidable succession of opponents – Jim Meadowcroft, Doug Mountjoy, Willie Thorne, Jimmy White, and finally Ray Reardon – to become World Champion for the second time. Meanwhile Alex had competed in *Pot Black* 82, winning just one game, against Cliff Thorburn.

In his year as the reigning World Champion, Alex found it difficult, if not impossible, to consolidate that position. His only major victory was in the Irish Professional Championship, and he was the losing finalist in the Lang's Scottish Masters and the Coral UK. His path to the semi-finals of the 1983 World Championship was relatively smooth – victories over Dean Reynolds, Willie Thorne and Bill Werbeniuk – but, in the 31-frame semi-final Alex managed to win only 5 against Steve Davis's 16.

Alex continued to attract his faithful followers throughout the 1983–4 season and in gaining the 1984 Coral UK title gave them full value for money. Trailing 7–0 to Steve Davis in the Final, Alex levelled the frame scores at 11–11, going on to 15–15 and winning the last frame 77–0. Davis subsequently beat Higgins 6–4 in the semi-finals of the Benson and Hedges Irish Masters and Alex failed to make his presence felt in *Pot Black* 84. In the 1984 World Championship the odd vital frame this time went against Alex, and the No.5 seed lost 10–9 to young Neal Foulds in the first round. The 1984–5 rankings list places the 'People's Champion' in ninth position.

Tony Knowles

Born in Bolton, Lancashire, in 1955, Tony has been playing snooker since the age of nine. His father was a steward at the Tonge Moor Conservative Club where the young Tony managed to practise on the club's full-sized table. He was a proficient player by the age of sixteen and met and played his idol, Alex Higgins, in occasional exhibition matches. Tony went to art college where he qualified as a graphic artist but upon leaving at the age of eighteen he decided upon a full-time snooker career. He won the British Junior Under 19 Championship twice – in 1972 and 1974 – and later represented England in Home International Team matches. He was the 'hero' of the winning England side in 1979, losing only two frames out of fifteen and receiving the 'Player of the Series' Award. Also in 1979 he first had individual successes, winning three important amateur tournaments including a £1000 first prize in the Pontin's autumn festival.

Tony turned professional at the beginning of 1980 but was too late to qualify for that year's World Championship. After a patient year of waiting and exhibition matches, Tony entered his first World Championship in 1981 but was knocked out, 10–8, in the first round by Graham Miles. He at last achieved a modest triumph and public recognition during the TV transmissions from the Coral UK Professional Championship at Preston. His 9–6 defeat of Doug Mountjoy and subsequent own defeat by 9–5 against Terry Griffiths in the quarter-finals were seen by millions of viewers, thus partially answering Tony's previous complaint: 'What I need is some television exposure.'

And there was to be more. Tony started the 1982 World Championship as a 150-1 'outsider', having to win his qualifying game against Eugene Hughes (Dublin) to reach the first round. The first session of the first round found Tony drawn against the defending champion, Steve Davis, the odds-on favourite. Davis, inexplicably, was completely off form, and again millions of viewers watched with disbelief as Tony Knowles defeated him by 10 frames to 1. It was a well-deserved win for Tony, who played with confidence and skill throughout. He went on to take his second-round match, 13–7, from Graham Miles but, in the quarter-finals for the first time in his career, eventually lost, 13–11, to Eddie Charlton.

Tony was selected as a member of the England team in the 1982 State Express World Team Classic in which he, Steve Davis and Jimmy White were the runners-up to Canada. A losing quarter-finalist in the Lang's Scottish Masters, Tony found the flavour of the Jameson Whiskey International more to his taste, defeating Eddie Sinclair in the first round, Ray Reardon in the second, Cliff Wilson in the quarter-finals and Kirk Stevens in the semis. His victory by 9 frames to 6 over David Taylor in the Final included a break of 114, the highest in the tournament. This earned Tony a total of £23,200, the highest individual prize of the year outside the World Championship. No other major titles came his way although he competed in many important events, but the 1983 World Championship saw Tony at his best again. As the fifteenth seed he beat Graham Miles, Ray Reardon and Tony Meo, but then unluckily lost by the odd frame, 16–15, to Cliff Thorburn in the semi-finals. Tony played in his first *Pot Black* series in 1983 and again in 1984 without reaching the final stages. He defeated Joe Johnson of Bradford in the untelevised Final of the 1983 Professional Players Tournament at Bristol.

Tony was a losing semi-finalist to Terry Griffiths in the 1984 Benson and Hedges Masters and runner-up to Steve Davis in the Tolly Cobbold Classic. These results, together with other consistent performances, earned Tony over £50,000 in prize-money for the year! Tony started as the number four seed for the 1984 World Championship during which he enjoyed some dubious press publicity but, perhaps, created more pertinent headlines by his shock defeat, 10–7, by former *Junior Pot Black* Champion John Parrott in the first round. Tony, whose hobbies include golf, tennis and squash, has, however, risen to second place in the World Ranking List.

Perrie Mans

The South African Snooker Champion from Johannesburg was invited to make his first appearance in *Pot Black* for the 1977 series. Perrie, whose actual name is Pierre, was one of the less fancied players in a line-up which included eleven other top-class professionals. His first game was against veteran Fred Davis which Perrie won by 66 points to 48. Next he beat Ray Reardon by 88 points to 42 and then Willie Thorne by 89 points to 42. It was now obvious that Perrie had taken the opportunity to become the first South African *Pot Black* Champion very seriously! Having now reached the Final, his opponent was another newcomer to the series, the Welsh player Doug Mountjoy. Showing almost complete indifference both to the television cameras and his rival, Perrie's determination to win was reflected in the result – Mans 90, Mountjoy 21. Perrie's score included a break of 59, the highest of the 1977 series.

One of the few left-handed players, Perrie had reached the quarter-finals of the 1974 World Championship by beating John Spencer. He defeated Graham Miles to reach the semi-finals in 1976 but, at Sheffield in 1977, Perrie was unable to survive the first round, losing to Dennis Taylor by 13–11. It was a different story when he returned to the Crucible Theatre one year later for, en route to the Final, he defeated the current World Champion John Spencer by 13 frames to 8. Perrie's next victim was Graham Miles 13–7, followed by a victory over Fred Davis in the semi-finals with the score at 18–16.

The marathon Final, watched by millions of *Grandstand* viewers, was against Ray Reardon, and although Perrie led at one stage by 18 frames to 17 he then succumbed to the Welshman's superior skill and experience. Perrie had to be content with the runner-up prize with the final score Reardon 25, Mans 18.

Perrie returned to the 1979 *Pot Black* team to retrieve the Trophy he had won in 1977. His first three games, against Doug Mountjoy, Fred Davis and Steve Davis, were all won convincingly and Perrie proceeded to the semi-finals without having lost a frame in two series! But here his run came to an end when his opponent in the 1978 World Championship Final, Ray Reardon, won 78–41. After an unsuccessful first round in the Holsten Lager International, Perrie's next major tournament was the Benson and Hedges Masters, held at the Wembley Conference Centre. In turn he defeated Cliff Thorburn, Ray Reardon and, in the Final, Alex Higgins to take the £3000 first prize.

The 1979 World Championship at Sheffield, in which Perrie was the No.2 seed, ended in the first round, when he lost to the eventual champion, Terry Griffiths, 8–13.

Snooker exists in South Africa mainly as an amateur sport. Until recently, Perrie has been offered little match-play experience or opposition in his own country. The situation has now dramatically changed since more of his fellow countrymen have been accepted into the professional ranks. In 1979 Jimmy van Rensburg, Derek Mienie and Roy Amdor became professionals with the almost immediate result of Perrie losing his South African Champion's title! He was beaten, 9–3, in the semi-finals by Mienie, who then defeated van Rensburg in the Final, 9–6.

Perrie was a member of the unsuccessful 'Rest of the World' team for the State Express World Cup in the autumn of 1979 and later returned to the Midlands to compete in his third *Pot Black* series, where one win, against Doug Mountjoy, was not enough for him to reach the semi-finals. But Perrie's next tournament was more rewarding when he gained £1000 as the runner-up to Alex Higgins in the Final of the Padmore/Super Crystalate International.

The next time that these two players met was in the Benson and Hedges Masters at Wembley Conference Centre, with Higgins winning again, by 5 frames to 1. In the 1980 World Championship, Perrie was seeded No.8 and his first game in the second round was, unfortunately for the South African, against – Alex Higgins! The result was a further win for Higgins by 13 frames to 6. Seeded 7 in the 1981 World Championship, Perrie again exited in the second round by a margin of 13 frames to 5 against 'Big' Bill Werbeniuk. He had previously scored a slightly unexpected success, beating Steve Davis 5–3 in the first round of the Benson and Hedges Masters, but his quarter-final game was a 5–4 failure against Cliff Thorburn.

In the 1982 World Championship the South African won his first round match, 10–8, against the unseeded Tony Meo, but followed it with a 13–6 defeat by Jimmy White. Perrie lost 5–2 to Kirk Stevens in the second round of the Jameson International later in the year, and 5–4 to Mark Wildman in the same round of the Professional

Players Tournament. Another second-round defeat was delivered by Kirk Stevens, 13–3, in the 1983 World Championship. In the interim, Perrie had the satisfaction of winning his eighteenth South African Professional Championship, 11–7, against Silvino Francisco, netting £5000.

Recently Perrie and Silvino have been joined by two more South African players, Mike Hines and François Ellis, who have been granted professional status in the UK by the WPBSA.

Perrie's visits to the UK have now become infrequent, partly as a result of increased numerical competition from his colleagues and partly because any prize-money he wins is offset by air-fares and other expenses. Although he did return to play in the 1984 World Championship, it was only to suffer a crushing defeat by John Parrott, 10–0, in the qualifying round. Hopefully, the quiet, likeable South African will find more lucrative opportunities in the future.

Tony Meo

The 1978 Junior Snooker Champion, christened Anthony Christian Meo by his Italian parents, was born in London in October 1959. Tony began to show signs of obvious ability at snooker when he started to play the game at the age of thirteen. 'After a year or so,' he says, 'people told me that I should take it up seriously.' Which is what Tony did, and by 1977 he had won several amateur championships, including the Tirfor and the Warner's Pro-Am.

The last few years have seen Tony really make his presence felt on the snooker circuit. At Prestatyn in May 1978 he was narrowly beaten 7–6 by Steve Davis in the Pontin's Open Championship. At Leeds he took the title of Junior Snooker Champion from Ian Williamson, who had held it for two years. His outstanding performance of the year, however, was in Toronto, Canada, when he competed in the Canadian Open Championship and won his way into the Final against Cliff Thorburn, having defeated Alex Higgins in the semi-finals. Although Meo lost 17–15, he showed that he is one of the most promising young players in the country. He was runner-up to Mike Hallett of Grimsby in the 'Pot Red' tournament at Wembley in

December 1978, which featured eight of the top teenage snooker players. He reached the quarter-finals of the English Amateur Snooker Championship (Southern Section) in 1979 but did not reproduce his best form on this occasion, losing 4–2.

At the age of seventeen Tony was the youngest player ever to score a 147 break – against Terry Whitthread at the Pot Black Snooker Centre in Clapham. In the summer of 1979 he set up another record by being accepted as a professional player at the age of nineteen. One of his first major tournaments was the 1979 Coral UK, where he beat Manchester's David Taylor by 9–7 before losing to the eventual champion, John Virgo. In the British Gold Cup he defeated Steve Davis, Roy Andrewartha and Doug Mountjoy before losing to Alex Higgins in the semi-finals. Tony had to qualify from 'scratch' in the 1980 World Championship which he did with an impressive win over Jimmy van Rensburg (South Africa) by 9 frames to 1. His first-round game was one of his best performances so far, losing by just one frame, 10–9, to Alex Higgins once again.

The 1980 Coral UK ended for Tony in the quarter-finals where he lost 9–5 to Steve Davis, who also beat him 9–3 in the Final of the John Courage English Professional Championship. Tony was also going strong in the 1981 World Championship, where he made a break of 134 against John Virgo in the first round, winning 10 frames to 6, before he met Terry Griffiths in the second round, losing by 13–6.

Tony beat Alex Higgins, 6–1, in the Final of the 1981 Lucania Professional Championship, and in Australia he won the Winfield Masters – their television equivalent to *Pot Black*. In the 1982 Benson and Hedges Masters he beat David Taylor and Cliff Thorburn, earning a place in the semi-finals. Although he lost to his stable-mate, Steve Davis, he had the distinction of scoring the highest break in the competition – 136.

Starting as the eighteenth seed for the 1982 World Championship, Tony lost to Perrie Mans, 10–8, in the first round, and made an even earlier retreat when beaten by Eddie Sinclair (Glasgow) in the qualifying rounds of the Jameson International. He made little show in the Professional Players tournament with a third-round defeat by Eddie Charlton, but an improved performance in the Coral UK Championship took him to the semi-finals where he lost 9–7 to Terry Griffiths. Success, albeit shared with Steve Davis, finally came Tony's way in winning the Hofmeister World Doubles, and making the highest break of 124 into the bargain. The left-hander also won two Irish tournaments – the Coleraine Top 4 competition and the St Comgalls Masters.

In three following major tournaments he lost 5–3 to Eddie Charlton in the first round of the Benson and Hedges, and was a losing quarter-finalist in both the Yamaha International and the Benson and Hedges Irish Masters. Although a beaten quarter-finalist, too, in the 1983 World Championship, Tony had produced snooker of a much higher quality. Before losing to Tony Knowles, 13–9, he had battled his way through the earlier rounds against Vic Harris, Geoff Foulds, Jimmy White and Doug Mountjoy. Tony celebrated during the Pontin's Festival at Brean Sands with a 'double' – a victory in the Pairs with his pal Jimmy White and in the Professional Final against Silvino Francisco. Overseas success followed when he toured South-East Asia, winning the Bangkok Golden Tournament and a '*Pot Black*-type' television event.

78   Tony finished the 1983–4 season high up on the list of

top money-makers. His main successes were in the State Express World Team Classic (with Steve Davis and Tony Knowles), the Hofmeister World Doubles Championship (joint winner with Steve Davis) and the Lada Classic, where he was beaten 9–8 by Steve Davis in the Final. His highest break of 139 in the Coral UK was also worth £1000! Perhaps tony's biggest disappointment came in the first round of the 1984 World Championship where, contrary to form, he lost 10–5 to Silvino Francisco. He had previously lost to Eddie Charlton in the new-style 'knock-out' frames in *Pot Black* 84. Tony has now risen four places in the ranking list to No.11.

Graham Miles

Birmingham's own snooker star made a quiet but effective entry into the professional scene. Graham had won several minor tournaments in the Midlands but he really came to prominence in 1973 when he reached the World Championship quarter-finals before losing to Eddie Charlton. However, this performance and a growing public reputation led to Miles being invited to play in the 1974 series of *Pot Black*. In the three-frame Final, Graham won against John Spencer by taking the first two frames and scoring the highest break in the competition. A few weeks later he maintained this form and reached the Final of the 1974 World Championship. On this occasion he was unable to cope with the opposition from Ray Reardon who was defending his world title. Graham lost, 22–12, but had nearly brought off a remarkable 'double'.

The 1975 *Pot Black* competition once again included Graham and he proved that his previous success on the programme was no fluke. He defeated Ray Reardon in his first game by a large margin, and then Eddie Charlton, before losing to John Spencer. These victories were sufficient to get himself into the semi-finals where he had a narrow win over Reardon. The Final against Dennis Taylor saw Graham the *Pot Black* Champion for the second year in succession.

Pot Black 78 celebrated its tenth year on BBC2 and Graham was undefeated until he met Doug Mountjoy in the Final. He took the first frame but with Doug in superlative form the Midlander finished as runner-up.

Twelve months later these two players met yet again in the first semi-final of *Pot Black* 79. Graham had won against Eddie Charlton and John Spencer to improve his chances of winning the Championship for the third time. Mountjoy ended his hopes by taking the game by 77 points to 40 with Graham gracious in defeat. It was this sporting spirit displayed by Miles which contributed to the decision to present him with the *Pot Black* Personality Award at the end of the series. He later competed in an invitation tournament at the Bombay Gymkhana taking the third prize with victories over Patsy Fagan and Dennis Taylor. The Midlander lost to Ray Reardon in the first round of the 1979 World Championship – a game where he was handicapped by a severe attack of flu.

Graham, who is the manager of a building company in Birmingham, has always been known for his unorthodox style of 'sighting' with the cue rubbing the left-hand side of his chin. It is believed that he is now trying to change his stance to a more conventional form. Meanwhile, the old style has produced two maximum breaks of 147 and in the 1978 UK Championship he scored a break of 139, a record for the event.

Graham's name didn't figure too prominently in the results lists of 1980's important tournaments. He represented England in the State Express World Cup where his team was beaten in the Final by Wales, Graham losing to Terry Griffiths and Doug Mountjoy. In *Pot Black* 80 his one success was over Perrie Mans by 93 points to 18, when he cleared the table with a magnificent break of 68. But he was disappointing in the Padmore/Super Crystalate International against Willie Thorne and against John Spencer in the Wilson's Classic; a 9–5 defeat by Patsy Fagan put him out of the Coral UK, and he made an early exit from the British Gold Cup in a Group 3 play-off against Tony Meo. His fortunes were no better in the 1980 World Championship, suffering another defeat, 10–3, by the young Canadian Kirk Stevens in the first round.

During the 1980–1 season Graham's programme included the Champion of Champions where he beat Alex Higgins 5–4 but failed to qualify in his group. He lost to Eddie Sinclair (Glasgow) in the first round of the Coral UK, and to Cliff Thorburn in the second round of the World Championship. But a much overdue success materialised for the Midlander in the Tolly Cobbold

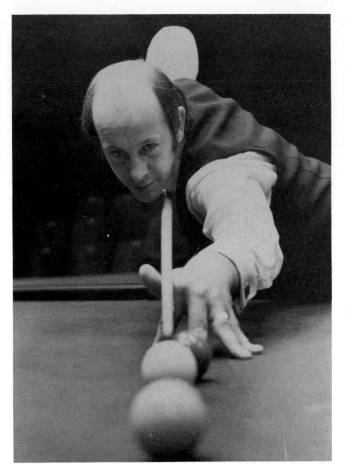

Classic in February 1981, when Graham produced his best form for some time to score a convincing win against Cliff Thorburn in the Final by 5 frames to 1 and take the £2000 first prize.

No other major prizes have come Graham's way since, although he got to the Tolly Cobbold semi-finals again in 1982, losing to Steve Davis on this occasion. He competed in the Yamaha Organs and again went out in the Group B semi-finals. His form in the 1982 World Championship was only moderate and, after a first-round win over Dave Martin, he was beaten, 13–7, by Tony Knowles, fresh from his victory over Steve Davis. The 1982–3

81

season also brought little reward. Graham had added to his business ventures the management of a new West Midlands snooker centre, concentrating less on tournament play. He failed to qualify for the 1982 Jameson International and was knocked out of the Professional Players Tournament 5–1 by Joe Johnson and the Coral UK 9–4 by Tony Meo. The Midlander's luck deserted him again in the 1983 World Championship when, for the second year running, he was beaten by Tony Knowles, 10–3, in the first round.

Graham fared no better in the next twelve months, entering few of the big competitions. He lost 9–4 to Mike Hallett (Grimsby) in the first round of the Coral UK but, partnered by Australian George Ganim, survived the first round of the Hofmeister World Doubles, only to be disqualified from the second round due to a misunderstanding and his late arrival for the match. He did, however, qualify for the first round of the 1984 World Championship, where he had been a finalist in 1974, but lost on this occasion to former World Champion John Spencer by 10 frames to 3.

Doug Mountjoy

Doug's snooker career from his amateur days to joining the professional ranks bears a strong resemblance to that of his fellow Welshman Ray Reardon. Both are ex-miners and former Welsh Amateur Snooker Champions. Doug's name first appeared in the record books in 1966 as the runner-up for the Welsh Amateur Championship. He won the title in 1968 and again in 1976. During this period he also represented Wales in the International Tournaments and won against Patsy Fagan (Ireland) and John Virgo (England). The World Amateur Snooker Championship was held at the President Hotel, Johannesburg, in October 1976 with some of the games shown on the new South African television service. Twenty-four players competed and Doug, playing in Group One, won all his seven games and fought his way to the Final. His opponent, Paul Mifsud from Malta, managed to win just one frame out of twelve!

The new World Amateur Champion was then invited to

play in *Pot Black* and Mountjoy decided to turn professional. His first appearance in *Pot Black* saw him reach the 1977 Final, but he was given little chance by Perrie Mans. Nevertheless, Doug had justified his inclusion in the series and was satisfied with his decision to become a professional.

This confidence and optimism was confirmed when, in early 1977, Doug met Ray Reardon in the Final of the Benson and Hedges Masters Tournament at the London Theatre, Drury Lane. Doug had already beaten John Pulman, Fred Davis and Alex 'Hurricane' Higgins to qualify and he went on to further victory with a 7 frames to 6 win against Reardon. Later that year Doug was knocked out in the quarter-finals of the World Championship by Dennis Taylor, and in 1978 lost to Ray Reardon in the first round.

Meanwhile, Doug had played again in his second *Pot Black*, losing to Ray Reardon but winning against Alex Higgins and Dennis Taylor. He was then in the Final for the second year running, and won two of the three frames against Graham Miles, including the highest break of 101, earning the title of *Pot Black* Champion 1978.

Only a few weeks before returning to the *Pot Black* studios to defend his title in the 1979 series, he competed in the UK Professional Championship at the Guild Hall, Preston. The Tournament, sponsored by Corals, saw Doug defeat Dennis Taylor, Roy Andrewartha, Graham Miles and (in the Final) David Taylor, to achieve yet another important snooker honour. The new UK Champion then played in his third series of *Pot Black*. With victories over Steve Davis and Graham Miles he reached the Final for the third year in succession. On this occasion Ray Reardon beat him 2–1. Mountjoy, however, once again won the Highest Break prize and the Joe Davis Trophy with a score of 82.

Doug subsequently took his revenge when he defeated Reardon in the Final of the Benson and Hedges Masters Tournament played in Ireland. Although unseeded, he was one of the more fancied players to win the 1979 World Championship at Sheffield. However, after winning his two qualifying matches Doug lost to Eddie Charlton in the first round. The next major competition for Doug was held at the scene of some of his earlier triumphs, the Pontin's Snooker Festival at Prestatyn. Doug had, as an amateur, twice won the Pontin's Open, and on this occasion, playing against his professional colleagues, he emerged the winner in the Final against Graham Miles. Later in 1979 he was a member of a formidable Welsh trio in the State Express World Challenge Cup. With Terry Griffiths and Ray Reardon, he formed an unbeatable combination who easily defeated England 14–3 in the Final, sharing the first prize of £7500.

Doug's attempt to win the Coral UK title for the second year running ended in the second round when he lost to Steve Davis by 9 frames to 5. The Woodpecker Welsh Professional Championship, held at the Leisure Centre in his home-town of Ebbw Vale, featured Doug, Ray Reardon, Terry Griffiths and Cliff Wilson. It was a triumph for Doug with victories over Terry Griffiths and then the title-holder, Ray Reardon, in the Final. He therefore approached the 1980 World Championship with a certain degree of confidence, having beaten the 1978 and 1979 World Champions! His first opponent was Cliff Wilson, whom he beat by 10 frames to 6. He then found himself drawn against the eventual winner, Cliff Thorburn, in the next round. This game resulted in a 13–10 defeat after Doug had levelled the score at 10–10 at one stage, making a break of 123 in the last session. In *Pot Black* 80 Doug reached the semi-finals yet again, but was beaten by Ray Reardon. In the 'play-off' with Dennis Taylor, Doug won to earn a third place in the competition.

The New London Theatre was the setting for two of Doug's successes in the autumn of 1980. In October he won the title of 'Champion of Champions' after a round-robin contest in which he defeated John Virgo in the Final by 10 frames to 8. Then within a fortnight, Doug, Ray Reardon and Terry Griffiths – the Welsh team – won the State Express World Cup for the second year in succession. Doug's own moments of glory, though, were to be in the 1981 World Championship at Sheffield. His break of 145 against Ray Reardon in the semi-finals earned him £1200 for the highest break in the tournament plus £5000 for the record break in the history of the Championship. Seeded 14, he fought his way to the Final with victories against Willie Thorne, Eddie Charlton, Dennis Taylor and Ray Reardon. Doug's ultimate disappointment, losing 18–12 to Steve Davis, was at least partially compensated by the additional £10,000 he received as the runner-up.

The 1981–2 season continued as busily as ever for Doug – the Jameson International, where he suffered a 5–1 defeat by Alex Higgins in the third round; the Coral UK, beaten by Tony Knowles, 9–6, also in the third round; the Northern Ireland Classic, losing 9–8 to Jimmy White in the semi-finals; and of course *Pot Black* 82. After being a 'group loser' in the Yamaha Organs Trophy, Doug put in some hard practice, which paid rapid dividends – £5000 as the winner of the Woodpecker Welsh Professional Championship, his second success in this competition in three years. Next was the 1982 World Championship, where he first beat Rex Williams comfortably, 10–3, then lost to Alex Higgins in the second round by the narrowest of margins – 13–12.

Between the 1982 and 1983 World Championships Doug produced a stream of steady if not spectacular performances. They included reaching the quarter-finals of the Lada Classic, the semi-finals of the Benson and Hedges Masters, runner-up to Ray Reardon in the Woodpecker Welsh Championship, and a semi-final group loser in the Yamaha International. In the 1983 World Championship itself Doug started as the seventh seed, but lost 13–11 to Tony Meo in the second round. Long-overdue success finally arrived at Prestatyn in the summer of 1983 where he turned the tables on Ray Reardon, to win the Pontin's Professional Tournament by 9 frames to 7. Some weeks later and several thousand miles away – in Hong Kong – Doug won the Camus Masters Tournament, 4–3, against Terry Griffiths.

Doug shared the runner-up prize-money in the State Express World Team Classic when Wales were beaten by England and lost to Tony Knowles in the second round of the Coral UK. Following some below-par performances in the Lada Classic, the Benson and Hedges Masters and the Yamaha International, victory came at last for Doug when he won the Welsh Professional Championship for the third time, beating Clive Everton, Terry Griffiths and, in the Final, Cliff Wilson. Doug also played well in the 1984 World Championship and on his way to the quarter-finals had defeated two young promising professionals, Mike Hallett and Neal Foulds. But his opponent in the quarter-finals, Dennis Taylor, played even better and defeated Doug 13 frames to 8. The Welsh Champion lost his 'knock-out' frame, 81–40, to his fellow countryman Terry Griffiths in *Pot Black* 84 where Doug was making his sixth appearance in the series. Doug is now ranked fifteen in the official list.

John Parrott

John Parrott was born in 1964 in Liverpool. He is a former North West Junior Champion and runner-up in the British Junior Under 16 and Under 19 Championships. John made his television début on *Junior Pot Black* in 1981, taking the highest break prize with a score of 98. In 1982 he won the Pontin's Open Tournament, beating Ray Reardon in the Final, and became the *Junior Pot Black* Champion that year and again in 1983. He also won the Zimbabwe Open in 1982 and 1983. Before turning professional in 1983, John was the losing finalist in the BCE English Amateur Championship, later signing a lucrative contract to endorse cues for a well-known manufacturer.

In his first year on the professional circuit, John and his new managers have had good reason to be pleased with themselves. In the 1984 Lada Classic, the tall young Liverpudlian defeated Doug Mountjoy, Alex Higgins and Tony Knowles to reach the semi-finals. John lost by one frame, 5–4, to Steve Davis but won £7000 for his efforts. Entering the World Championship for the first time John repeated his 'giant-killing' to get through to the second round. His victims were Dennis Hughes (Manchester), Clive Everton and Perrie Mans (10–0). In the first round he again defeated Tony Knowles by 10 frames to 7. Although John lost 13–11 to Dennis Taylor in the second round, he still has enough time on his side to become the world's youngest-ever champion! He also qualifies to compete in *Pot Black* 85 and attempt to win the 'senior' championship.

Ray Reardon

The 1978 World Professional Snooker Champion was born in Tredegar, South Wales, on 8 October 1932. The young Ray inherited his love of snooker from his father and his uncles, all miners, and at the age of fourteen he too was working in the pits. Reardon became the Welsh Amateur Snooker Champion in 1950 and held this title until 1956.

After a near-fatal pit accident, he eventually left the mining industry and joined the Stoke-on-Trent Constabulary. He quickly established himself as the Police Snooker Champion and went on to win the English Amateur Championship from another famous player – John Spencer.

Turning professional, Reardon held the World Championship from April to November 1970. In the 75-frame Final at the City Hall, Manchester, in April 1973 he beat Eddie Charlton to win the Championship for the second time. Just twelve months later, back in Manchester at Belle Vue, he won his third title with a comparatively easy victory over the 1974 *Pot Black* Champion, Graham Miles, 22–12.

The 1975 World Championship, played in Australia, extended Reardon to the full and this time it was no walkover for him. In the Final against Eddie Charlton in Sydney Ray won by just one frame! In 1976, however, back in Manchester he won his fifth title comparatively easily.

The 1977 World Championship was staged at the Crucible Theatre in Sheffield. Reardon won his first-round match against Patsy Fagan comfortably enough by 13 frames to 7 but in the quarter-finals the defending champion met John Spencer and, obviously nowhere near his best form, was beaten 13 frames to 6.

His return to glory took just twelve months and happened at the same venue. He regained the World title, his sixth, beating the Australian Eddie Charlton in the semi-finals and South African Perrie Mans in the Final.

With the exception of 1971, when Reardon was touring South Africa, he has competed in every *Pot Black* series to date and won the first Trophy in 1969. He was the losing finalist in 1970 and 1972, and in 1975 he beat Fred Davis in the 'play-off' for the special prize for third place in the tournament.

One of Ray's major successes in 1978 was in the *Daily Mirror* 'Champion of Champions' Tournament at the Wembley Conference Centre, where he beat Alex Higgins 11–9, to win the first prize of £2000. Ray carried this form forward shortly after to the recordings of the 1979 *Pot Black* competition. He won his first game against John Spencer, lost to Eddie Charlton and then defeated Graham Miles, Perrie Mans and Doug Mountjoy to become *Pot Black* Champion for the second time.

Ray's downfall, brought about by Dennis Taylor in the quarter-finals of the 1979 World Championship, was the biggest upset of the tournament. The reigning World Champion had started, as No.1 seed, a warm favourite to win the title for the seventh time. His first game, against Graham Miles, was won comfortably enough, 13–8, but a seeming loss of concentration in the quarter-finals contributed to his departure from the championship stakes with Dennis Taylor winning this time, also 13–8.

Ray shared the first prize with Terry Griffiths and Doug Mountjoy when Wales won the State Express World Challenge Cup at Haden Hill in the autumn of 1979.

However, he was less pleased when a few weeks later Mountjoy deprived him of the Welsh Professional Champion title at Ebbw Vale! His eleventh appearance in *Pot Black* 80 began well, with three wins in a row against Terry Griffiths, John Spencer and Dennis Taylor. With a further win against Mountjoy in the semi-finals Ray was in the *Pot Black* Final once again, where his opponent was his old rival Eddie Charlton, who lost the first frame but took the next two leaving Ray with the runner-up prize for the third time in the programme's history.

Reardon's next main events were the Benson and Hedges Masters, where he lost to Alex Higgins in the semi-finals, and the 1980 World Championship. The six-times winner started favourite and kept his supporters happy, winning his first game against Bill Werbeniuk by 13 frames to 6. One of the biggest upsets of the tournament occurred in the quarter-finals, however, when David Taylor (a 66–1 outsider), put the ex-Champion out of the competition with a 13–11 victory.

The next twelve months were as busy as ever for Ray. He played in *Pot Black* 81 – his twelfth appearance in the series – and was unbeaten in his first three games against Cliff Thorburn, Steve Davis and Kirk Stevens, but lost to Jim Wych in the semi-finals and, eventually, to Eddie Charlton in the 'play-off' for third place in the competition. However, a major tournament that he did succeed in winning was the Woodpecker Welsh Professional Championship in February 1981 where he regained his title from Terry Griffiths and Cliff Wilson. Ray had previously, of course, represented the Welsh Team (with Terry Griffiths and Doug Mountjoy) which won the State Express World Cup in October 1980. In the 1981 World Championship itself, the former Champion again reached the semi-finals after scoring against John Spencer and Bill Werbeniuk. There Doug Mountjoy inflicted a 16–10 defeat on Ray during which Doug made a break of 145, at that time a record for the Championship.

Ray, one of the busiest and most consistent professionals, was presented with the *Pot Black* Personality Award at the end of the 1982 series. He won the Highland Masters at the Eden Court Theatre, Inverness, in April 1982 with a 6–0 victory over Steve Davis in the semi-finals and by 11–4 against John Spencer in the Final. His most notable achievement of the year was in reaching the final of the 1982 World Championship, where he lost to Alex Higgins by 18 frames to 15. Ray's next two Finals were in the Pontin's Open where, giving away 25 points per frame, he lost 7–4 to *Junior Pot Black* Champion John Parrott, and in the Pontin's Professional where he lost 9–4 to Steve Davis. He then lost to Terry Griffiths in the quarter-finals of the Lang's Scottish Masters and to Tony Knowles in the second round of the 1982 Jameson International, but regained his winning form by taking the first prize in the Professional Players Tournament with a 10–5 victory over Jimmy White. He lost to Alex Higgins in the semi-final of the Coral UK, was runner-up to Cliff Thorburn in the Benson and Hedges Masters Final, and then to Steve Davis in the Benson and Hedges Irish Masters Final.

Ray's two triumphs in the year were regaining the Woodpecker Welsh Professional Championship and the first prize of £12,000 in the Yamaha International Masters. He figured prominently, as ever, in the 1983 *Pot Black* series, and although beaten by Steve Davis in the Final he won the highest break prize with a score of 91. No doubt Ray's biggest disappointment of the season was in losing 13–12 to Tony Knowles in the second round of the 1983 World Championship.

Another busy season for Ray did not find him in the winners' enclosure in any major events, but there were some consolations. He captained Wales, the runners-up to England in the State Express World Team Classic, and was a quarter-finalist in the Benson and Hedges Masters. He competed in *Pot Black* 84 without reaching the closing stages but in the 1984 World Championship he won his first-round match against Jim Wych and the second round against Silvino Francisco. In the quarter-finals, however, Ray found no answer to the young Canadian Kirk Stevens, as the result shows – Stevens 13, Reardon 2.

Ray, who lives at Werrington near Stoke-on-Trent, is a keen golfer and has appeared on BBC TV's *Pro-Celebrity Golf* series. He was the first snooker player to be featured on *This is Your Life*, in 1976, and has subsequently had four books published. Ray is now ranked at number five.

HOW TO BECOME A TOP PLAYER
by Ray Reardon

I have entered championships both in England and Wales since the age of twelve. The first few years of participation in these events were purely to gain experience. Obviously, you always play to win; but at this age it is extremely useful to realise the feeling of playing before an audience. There is no substitute. Therefore, although winning is important, in losing you gain the drive to succeed the next time whilst learning to accept defeat gracefully.

To become a top player a great deal of sacrifice is necessary. It means playing in all of your spare time. Always enjoy playing but learn from your mistakes and, better still, always take full advantage of your opponent's errors.

You will discover that basically snooker is a game of *memory*. To remember how you played a particular shot in the past will enable you to recognise it when it occurs again in a similar situation and you will know how to cope with it.

Practise as often as is possible, but not to the point of boredom. Take part in every tournament that is open to you. Set yourself a goal and when it is yours take the next step up the ladder until you reach the top. When your ambition is finally achieved *practise some more*!

Method of play

I have never set out to play any game in a certain way even when the form of my opponent is well known to me. This is because each and every frame of snooker is different. After all, when the frame has begun, sometimes the black ball and a minor colour have been placed in a safe position which could result in the game being played defensively. Always play your own style of game – do not try to beat your opponent at his game. You may consider yourself to be a better potter than him and play all-attacking snooker – this is not good. When you alter your own game you create flaws in your style and will become vulnerable.

Make your own game as sound as you can in all the departments of potting, safety play and the art of playing snookers. Become the master of the cue-ball and you will, more easily, realise your ambitions.

SNOOKER CLINIC
by Ray Reardon

The 'End Game' of snooker is vital and therefore it is imperative that you are sure of potting the remaining balls, when 'on'.

In order to tighten this part of your game, I strongly recommend that you practise the following 'Snooker Clinic' to perfection. When satisfied, place the white (cue-) ball to your own chosen spot and practise.

Diagram 1
The cue-ball is set in the half-ball position to pot yellow ball into its own pocket. Strike the cue-ball at centre with enough strength to bring the cue-ball from the yellow ball onto the side cushion, then back into the centre of the table.

Diagram 2
Cue-ball is in a straight line with green ball. If we stop the cue-ball in place of green, a difficult shot on the brown follows. Therefore, cause the cue-ball to screw back a few inches to leave the brown ball easy. (Screw – this is done

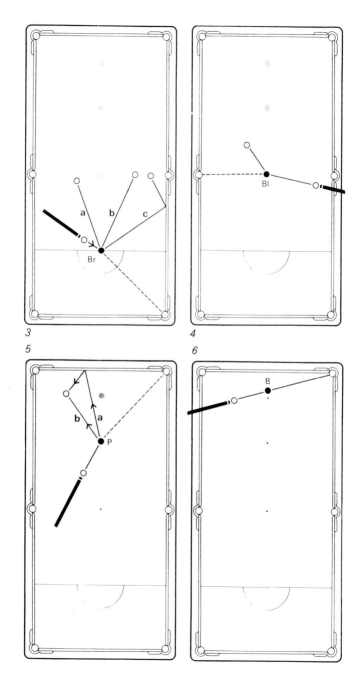

3

4

5

6

by striking the cue-ball three-quarters ball, which is between centre and table level, and sharp. Do not stab at the cue-ball, follow through with the cue.)

Diagram 3
This is an interesting shot, because we have three ways in which to play it and all three ways are correct.
'A' with deep screw, as described in Diagram 2, but played *very sharp.*
'B' again with screw, but this time with slight screw, so ease off with the sharpness.
'C' – stun shot. Strike cue-ball just below centre firmly. This causes the cue-ball to bounce away from the brown ball on to the side cushion, then off again.

Diagram 4
Strike cue-ball at centre, nice and slow, which leaves natural position.

Diagram 5
Two ways. Either, 'A', strike cue-ball at centre and roll through on to cushion, then off again, or, 'B', use slight screw, as Diagram 3 at 'B'.

Diagram 6
Pot black the easy way. Remember, never mind how the black is potted, you can only win once, so make it easy. Nothing fancy, please – no exhibition stuff. Just be sure and win.

   N.B. It will be noted that I have made no mention of the use of *side* when striking the cue-ball. This has been omitted intentionally, because its use can cause complications and the 'Clinic' is to assist the beginner.

Dean Reynolds

One of *Junior Pot Black*'s 'discoveries', Dean comes from Grimsby and was born in January 1963. He became interested in snooker at the age of five at his father's club, and began beating the senior members by the time he was twelve. In 1979 he won the Grimsby Boys Snooker Championship and the Lincs/South Humberside Junior Championship. By the end of 1980 Dean had made over fifty century breaks, including a personal best of 143.
   His first appearance on television was in the 1981 series

95

of *Junior Pot Black*, becoming the winner of the new trophy. He then went on to win the British Junior Under 19 Championship and turned professional in the autumn of 1981.

Playing in his first World Championship in 1982, the *Junior Pot Black* Champion put up a very creditable performance. He won his first two qualifying games against two experienced players – Dessie Sheehan (Dublin) and former World Amateur Champion Ray Edmonds (Cleethorpes). Dean then won his first-round match against the oldest and most experienced competitor in the tournament, Fred Davis, by 10 frames to 7. In the second round his opponent was the little-known South African Champion, Silvino Francisco, and Dean was not disgraced in losing by 13 frames to 8.

In his first full year as a professional Dean made moderate but promising progress. His best performances were in the Jameson International, beating Willie Thorne in the first round 5–3, and reaching the quarter-finals of the Professional Players Tournament. He also had a narrow defeat, 9–8, against Alex Higgins in the second round of the Coral UK. It was unfortunate for the young player that he met Higgins again in the first round of the 1983 World Championship where he lost by a wider margin of 10 frames to 4.

In Dean's third season as a professional it again proved difficult for him to achieve any notable successes. He failed to get past the opening stages of the Jameson International, the Lada Classic, the Yamaha International and the 1984 World Championship. In the Coral UK he lost to Paul Medati in the first round, 9–3, but, in partnership with Patsy Fagan, reached the second round of the Hofmeister World Doubles by defeating Ray Edmonds and Jim Meadowcroft. Reynolds and Fagan lost their next match 5–2 to the formidable duo John Virgo and Cliff Thorburn. Dean is no doubt discovering that life is 'tough at the top' for today's snooker professionals, providing that you can get there!

John Spencer

Manchester's snooker star John Spencer learned to play at a local Sunday school institute and made a break of 115 when he was just fifteen years old. Three years later, after considerable dedication to the game, Spencer began his National Service. It was ten years before he took up snooker seriously again and after a succession of matches playing for side-stakes he entered the English Amateur Championships and lost narrowly in the Final to Ray Reardon.

He eventually gained this amateur title in 1966, turning professional in the same year. The 1969 *Pot Black* series included the new World Champion, John Spencer, amongst the more established star performers and he reached the Final, where his opponent was Ray Reardon. Spencer lost this game, but gained his revenge by beating Ray Reardon and Fred Davis in the 1970 and 1971 *Pot Black* Finals respectively.

Meanwhile, Spencer had won the World Championship again – in November 1970 – only to relinquish it to Alex Higgins in 1972. Spencer has often figured prominently in the closing stages of *Pot Black*. Apart from his successes in 1970 and 1971, he scored the highest break in 1972 and was runner-up to Graham Miles in 1974. In superb form throughout the 1976 series, John defeated Dennis Taylor in the Final to become the first 'three-time' winner of the *Pot Black* Trophy.

John was the local favourite to win the 1976 World Championship which was held at his home town of Manchester, but his quarter-final match against Alex Higgins ended disappointingly for him and his supporters when Higgins won by 15 frames to 14. The 1977 World Championship at Sheffield found John with renewed stamina and confidence. His path to winning the World title for the third time was paved with victories over John Virgo, Ray Reardon, John Pulman and, in the Final, the Canadian Cliff Thorburn. John was beaten by Perrie Mans in the first round of the 1978 contest, but not before he had scored the highest break of the Championship. The magnificent break of 138 was witnessed by millions of BBC2 viewers.

John received the *Pot Black* Personality Award in 1978 for being the only player to have appeared in ten series on the programme and to have won the *Pot Black* Trophy on three occasions. The 1979 *Pot Black* competition, however, proved to be an unlucky one for him, with just one win, against Eddie Charlton, to his credit. Spencer's winning streak returned within a short while when he won the Holsten Lager International at the Fulcrum Centre, Slough. In beating Graham Miles in the final 11–7 John clinched the first prize of £3500. It was during the quarter-finals that he scored a maximum break of 147 against Cliff Thorburn and earned another £500 from the sponsors. However, had he made this break in another sponsored event the cheque would have been for £10,000!

Later in the year John, together with some of his colleagues, was invited to Bombay to compete in an International 'Round-Robin' Tournament, sponsored by a local paint company. At the finish John had won the first prize (£2000), the Highest Break prize with a score of 108 and the Man of the Series award.

Back at the Crucible Theatre in Sheffield for the 1979 World Championship (and where he had won the title in 1977), John began the competition as the second favourite. But he and his supporters were thwarted when he lost 13–11 to the burly Canadian Bill Werbeniuk in the

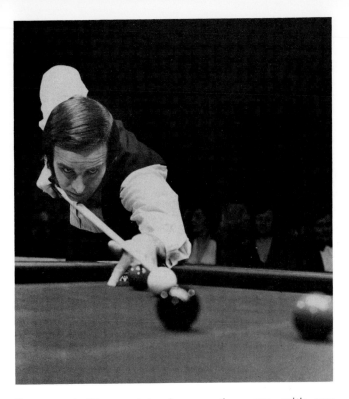

first round. The next twelve months were, with one exception, not particularly rewarding for John, although they were busy enough. He represented the English team (the runners-up) in the State Express World Cup and his other engagements included *Pot Black* 80, the Coral UK, the Padmore/Super Crystalate International, the British Gold Cup and the Benson and Hedges Masters. The former *Pot Black* Champion lost his three games in the 1980 series to Dennis Taylor, Ray Reardon and Terry Griffiths. It was Terry who also 'whitewashed' John 5–0 in the Benson and Hedges semi-finals.

John's major success was in the brewery-sponsored Wilson's Classic at the New Century Hall, Manchester, in January 1980. His victims were Graham Miles, John Virgo and, in the Final, Alex Higgins. John's 4–3 victory earned him the first prize of £3000 and it was his biggest financial gain since winning the Holsten Lager International the previous year. Following his defeat by Kirk

Stevens, 13–8, in the 1980 World Championship he was placed in fifteenth position in the World Ranking List.

Between then and the 1981 World Championship John produced little of his winning form in major events. The nearest he came to the big prize money was in the Benson and Hedges Masters in January 1981, where he met Terry Griffiths in the semi-finals and at the end of a long, hard-fought game the score was 6–5 to Griffiths. This effort, nevertheless, was worth £2000 to John. He began the 1981 World Championship by narrowly defeating Ray Edmonds in the first round, 10–9, and then faced his old colleague and perennial opponent Ray Reardon. The result – Reardon 13, Spencer 11 – was an indication of both the pressure of the game on the two adversaries and how much John's previous form had returned.

Later that year Ray and John were again in opposition as members of the Wales and England teams in the State Express World Team Classic Final. It was John's turn to be on the winning side and to share the £12,000 prize-money with Steve Davis and David Taylor. He played well below his best form in the 1982 World Championship, going out 13–5 against Willie Thorne in the second round, and continued the competition as one of the BBC commentary team!

In the 1982 Jameson International John lost 5–4 to John Virgo in the second round, and again lost to Virgo in the third round of the Professional Players Tournament. He reached the quarter-finals of the Coral UK, beating Eddie Sinclair and Tony Knowles before succumbing to Alex Higgins 9–5. John also partnered Ray Reardon in the Hofmeister World Doubles, where they were losing quarter-finalists. However, John's best efforts came later, in the Lada Classic, where he lost by one frame, 5–4, to Steve Davis in the semi-finals. Back at the Crucible Theatre for the 1983 World Championship his hopes of getting back his former title vanished when Eddie Charlton took their second-round match by 13 frames to 11.

John cued his way fairly unspectacularly through the 1983–4 tournament programme where his best effort was to reach the quarter-finals of the Benson and Hedges Masters, beating Cliff Thorburn 5–4 in the first round, and then losing to Terry Griffiths by the same score. Coincidentally, the same two players met in the Final of *Pot Black* 84, where Griffiths was also the winner by one frame. John beat Graham Miles 10–3 in the first round of the 1984 World Championship but after a second-round defeat, 10–5, by Steve Davis, he returned to his seat in the BBC commentary box. John is now at thirteenth position in the new ranking list.

HOW TO WIN GAMES
by John Spencer

During my few years as a snooker professional travelling around the clubs, I have been asked a variety of questions about the game. I think the most interesting is why players who have been making 50–60 breaks frequently never seem to improve to the century-break class. I believe the answer to this is also one of the main differences between the professional and the top amateurs, and that is the mental attitude to the game. Obviously one of the reasons for this is that probably the professional has the ability to hold his concentration for long periods far better than most amateurs, but, this apart, it is reasonable to assume that a 60-break player can play most of the shots that a professional can play.

The basic mechanics of the game, once having been acquired, are only affected by one's own state of mind. Positive thinking produces positive play. As long as you think aggressively and positively you are mentally attuned to winning games, whereas if you continually think defensively, you are merely trying to avoid defeat.

A typical example of this attitude is shown when a player is left a longish straight red with all the other reds in a safe position. He will invariably get down and knock the red in nine times out of ten without even thinking. However, an identical shot with the remaining reds in such a position that his opponent will be left on if he misses the red will mean in some cases that he won't even attempt the red or miss the pot if he does. The reason for this is – he obviously isn't thinking positively; he is more concerned with what he is going to leave his opponent if he misses the pot and because of this his concentration is not entirely on the shot.

I think this attitude just about sums my game up. I have never been an admirer of the super tactician who, before a shot, weighs up all the possibilities and invariably prefers to wait for his opponent to make mistakes. Since I have been a professional I have always tried to be positive in my game, attacking whenever the opportunity arises. I don't believe in throwing my cue at everything in sight, but if, after weighing up the situation, I feel that it calls for aggression, I never hesitate. When I have made my mind up to go for a pot, I am concentrating a hundred per cent on the pot and never think what I will leave should I miss. Obviously, the amount of attacking a player does should depend on his own ability. Always play within your own limitations. If you are left a shot that you would normally knock in six times out of ten in practice, why refuse it because of the position of the other balls? After all, the percentage is that you will have six chances of winning to your opponent's four.

The best shots to go for are those which offer the maximum benefit when you get them and the least risk when you miss. The worst shots are those which offer the least benefit when you get them and the greatest risk when you miss. This is all part of the mental approach to the game, deciding when is the right time to attack.

Positive thinking also comes into safety play of course. Most players play a safety shot purely to stop their opponent from scoring, which can often be quite easy by running into the pyramid of reds, but this will leave your opponent a simple safety shot in return. Positive safety play is to try to put your opponent in the most awkward position from which to play a safety shot in return. Before playing your shot, study the position of the balls and decide the position that you would have most difficulty in escaping from, then try and put your opponent in the same spot.

Never begin a match with the thought that you have to win at all costs. This will put so much pressure on yourself that you will get tense even if things are going right for you and you won't be able to play your normal game. My own outlook is to play to the best of my ability and hope that it is good enough to win. Obviously I want to win as much as the next man, but I know it is not the end of the world if I lose. Believe it or not, I still get as much pleasure out of a game of snooker now as I did when I first started!

Kirk Stevens

'The Man in the White Suit' was one snooker columnist's description of Kirk Stevens, the young Canadian professional, when he appeared in the 1980 World Championship at Sheffield. He had, in fact, played in the same competition the year before without earning too much public recognition. Kirk was born in Toronto in August 1958. At the age of twelve he is said to have challenged Cliff Thorburn, then the resident professional at a billiard hall, to a game for two dollars! (Needless to add, Kirk lost.) Kirk, however, became a useful amateur player and in 1978 reached the semi-finals of the World Amateur Snooker Championship held in Malta. Although he was well beaten by Cliff Wilson 8–2, he decided to turn professional and his application was accepted in December 1978. In 1979 he won back his two dollars (with interest), by defeating Cliff Thorburn, the reigning champion, by 7 frames to 5 for the Canadian Championship.

Kirk's first entry into the World Championship was also in 1979. He won his first two qualifying games against Roy Amdor (South Africa) and John Pulman and was then beaten by the veteran Fred Davis, 13–8, in the first round. Later he played for the Canadian team in the State Express World Cup where he beat Ray Reardon and Gary Owen, making a 69 break against Reardon. In September 1979 he was home in Toronto for the Canadian International, beating Dennis Taylor in the quarter-finals and losing by one frame, 9–8, to Terry Griffiths in the semis.

The inaugural Canadian Professional Championship, sponsored by Dufferin Cues, was held in April 1980 when Kirk was beaten 9–7 by his young contemporary, Jim Wych, in the semi-finals. His second appearance in the World Championship, however, really brought him to the notice of the public, press and television viewers alike. He started quietly but successfully, with wins in the qualifying section over David Greaves and Mike Hallett. His first-round game was a decisive defeat of Graham Miles by 10 frames to 3, in which Kirk had a break of 136, tying with Steve Davis for the highest break in the Championship. In the second round the Canadian performed another 'giant-killing' act, disposing of John Spencer 13–8 with breaks of 91 and 88. His quarter-final game was against Eddie

Charlton and, with a confident win by 13 frames to 7, Kirk Stevens became the youngest player ever to enter the semi-finals. Kirk, whose style is similar at times to that of Alex Higgins, was now facing the 'Hurricane' himself and led 5–2 at the first interval, but gradually the strain of having played so many frames in a concentrated few days began to tell, and Higgins drew ahead to win 16–13.

By now Kirk's cheerful personality and talent had scored a hit with the British snooker-loving public and he was subsequently invited to play in *Pot Black* 81. He beat Steve Davis in his first game, but then lost to Cliff Thorburn and Ray Reardon. However, he did not leave the competition empty-handed, for during his game against Steve Davis his break of 79 won him the prize for the highest break in the series. The 1981 World Championship was not so fortunate for Kirk where he lost his second-round match against Dennis Taylor, 13–11, after winning 10–4 against John Dunning. Kirk was a losing semi-finalist to David Taylor in the Yamaha Organs Trophy at Derby and a losing quarter-finalist to Terry Griffiths in the Benson and Hedges Irish Masters, Dublin. As a member of the Canadian team for the 1980 State Express World Cup, Kirk again was on the losing side when Wales beat Canada in the Final.

Before the 1982 World Championship Kirk played little snooker and won less. He represented Canada again in the World Team Classic, together with Cliff Thorburn and Bill Werbeniuk, but his side lost to England in the semi-finals. He was beaten 5–0 by David Taylor in the third round of the Jameson and by Werbeniuk, 9–7, in the Coral UK. Kirk reproduced something near his best form at the Crucible Theatre, where he reached the quarter-finals of the 1982 World Championship. Seeded No. 10, the young Canadian was beaten 13–9 by the younger Londoner Jimmy White after wins against Jack Fitzmaurice and Patsy Fagan in the earlier rounds.

Together with Cliff Thorburn and Bill Werbeniuk, Kirk was at last on the winning side when the Canadian trio won the 1982 State Express World Team Classic. Kirk had previously been a losing semi-finalist in the Jameson International to the eventual winner, Tony Knowles. He later gained his revenge over Tony with a 5–0 victory in the quarter-finals of the Lada Classic and then lost his semi-final game against Bill Werbeniuk.

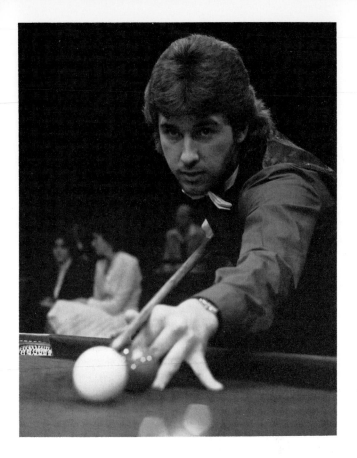

After making little impact in the Benson and Hedges Masters and the Yamaha International, Kirk, the sixth seed, was next engaged in the 1983 World Championship. He had an easy victory, 13–3, against Perrie Mans in the second round, but his quarter-final match against his 'master', Cliff Thorburn, resulted in one of the closest encounters in the classic event, with Thorburn winning 13–12.

Kirk's 1983–4 campaign was probably his best to date, despite competing unsuccessfully in *Pot Black* 83 and 84. He was a quarter-finalist in both the Professional Players Tournament and the Lada Classic. Although he was beaten 6–4 in the semi-finals of the 1984 Benson and Hedges Masters, one of his winning frames was composed of one single score – a 147 maximum! Kirk said afterwards: 'I couldn't believe how I felt. I was just enthralled . . .' So were millions of BBC TV viewers! He also made the highest break, 107, in the Yamaha International. In the 'fall' of 1983 Kirk had won the Canadian Professional Championship in Toronto, beating Frank Jonik 9–8. In the 1984 World Championship at Sheffield, Kirk was in sparkling form – he defeated the Scottish Champion, Eddie Sinclair, 10–1 in the first round, David Taylor 13–10 in the second and Ray Reardon 13–2 in the quarter-finals. Playing in his first ever World Championship semi-final, he and Jimmy White provided the most entertaining match of the competition. Both players deserved to win, but the final score was White 16 frames, Stevens 14. Kirk's position in the World Ranking List has now risen from seventh to fourth.

David Taylor

Another player born, bred and based in Manchester, in 1968 David Taylor won both the English Amateur Snooker Championship and the World Amateur Championship, held in Melbourne. It was not surprising that these feats prompted him to turn professional later that year. He was a member of the 1971 *Pot Black* team but, for a large part of his professional career, has enjoyed only moderate success on the tournament circuit. All his previous form was exceeded in the 1978 UK Championship at Preston where he started as one of the less fancied 'runners' and caused the major surprise of the competition by defeating Patsy Fagan, John Virgo and Alex Higgins before losing to Doug Mountjoy in the Final. In June 1978, he made three consecutive clearances with breaks of 130, 140 and 139 at Butlin's, Minehead; this is now recognised as a world record.

David's performances in the World Professional Championships until the spring of 1980 were modest, although he had twice reached the quarter-finals. He lost in the first round of the 1979 event to Alex Higgins, but 1980 was a different story. An easy win in the first round over Ray Edmonds (another former World Amateur Champion) was followed by a 13–5 victory against Fred Davis. Once again David was in the quarter-finals and facing the

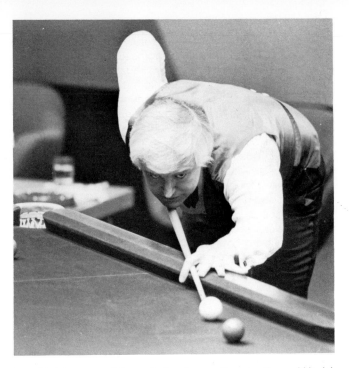

formidable opposition of the favourite, six-times World
Champion Ray Reardon. Playing his best snooker for
some years, David effected yet another reversal of form
which resulted in his winning by 13 frames to 11. He was
not disgraced in losing, in the semi-finals, to the eventual
World Champion of 1980, Cliff Thorburn. David thus
'jumped' from fifteenth to ninth position in the World
Rankings List, but, after the 1981 World Championship
where he reached the quarter-finals (losing to Cliff
Thorburn again), he was ranked No. 7. David returned to
Pot Black 81 after an absence of some ten years, but only
succeeded in winning one of his three qualifying frames.
A few weeks later, though, the 'Silver Fox' was at his peak
again and beat all but Steve Davis in the newly sponsored
Yamaha Organs Trophy. As runner-up he collected £5000
and the satisfaction of having beaten Doug Mountjoy,
Graham Miles and Kirk Stevens en route.

   A member of the victorious trio (with Steve Davis and
John Spencer) who won the 1982 World Team Classic,
David also played in *Pot Black* 82, beating Alex Higgins

but not qualifying for the semi-finals. He lost in the Group B semi-finals in the Yamaha Trophy, having previously beaten Cliff Thorburn, Alex Higgins and Tony Meo, and, surprisingly, failed against Patsy Fagan in the first round of the 1982 World Championship.

David provided his best performance for some time in the 1982 Jameson International, beating Mick Fisher, Bill Werbeniuk, Steve Davis and John Virgo. Although David had made a break of 101 in an earlier round, this was exceeded by his opponent in the Final, Tony Knowles, with 114. The result — Knowles 9, Taylor 6. The 'Silver Fox's' form in other major tournaments included a second-round defeat, 9–6, by Tony Meo in the Coral UK, reaching the quarter-finals of the Lada Classic, and a second-round defeat again, by Bill Werbeniuk, 13–10, in the 1983 World Championship.

Events really worked out no better for David in the next twelve months, more due to lack of confidence and concentration than ability. Runner-up in the 1982 Jameson International, he lost his qualifying game against Jim Donnelly (Glasgow) in the 1983 tournament. In the 1983 Coral UK David beat Neal Foulds 9–4 in the first round, losing 9–3 to Joe Johnson in the second. But David did not progress far in Benson and Hedges Masters, the Yamaha International or *Pot Black* 84. He lost 13–10 to Kirk Stevens in the second round of the World Championship having beaten another Canadian, Marcel Gauvreau, 10–5 in the first round. David, who was No.8 in the ranking list in 1982, has now dropped to sixteenth place.

Dennis Taylor

Dennis Taylor was invited to join the 1975 *Pot Black* team after his promising form both here and in Canada. At the age of twenty-five he was the youngest member of the team.

He learned to play the game in Coalisland, County Tyrone, and arrived in Darwen, Lancs, at the age of seventeen. He won the British Junior Billiards title in 1968 and was recognised as one of the most promising young professionals. Dennis lives in Blackburn and is married with two children.

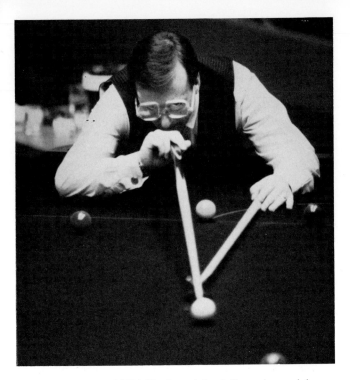

In September 1974 Taylor visited Canada and in an exhibition match in Toronto scored 349 points in three frames without missing a shot! 1975 was a successful year for the young Irishman: he reached the *Pot Black* Final at his first attempt and the semi-finals of the World Championship in Australia. Although defeated by Eddie Charlton, Taylor had, in turn, beaten Perrie Mans, Fred Davis and Gary Owen.

In 1976 he again reached the *Pot Black* Final, winning against Rex Williams, Willie Thorne and Fred Davis. However, John Spencer provided tougher opposition in the Final and Taylor, once more, had to be content with the runner-up prize.

Dennis competed in *Pot Black* in both 1977 and 1978 without reaching the closing stages but fared better in the 1977 World Championship. His victories over Perrie Mans and Doug Mountjoy earned him a place in the semi-finals for the second time in three years. However, although playing with great determination and confidence, he lost to Cliff Thorburn by 18 frames to 16.

As one of the members of the International 'Round Robin' Tournament played in Bombay in the spring of 1979, Dennis was the runner-up to John Spencer. He had been the only player to beat Spencer throughout the competition. The pinnacle of his career to date was reached at Sheffield in the World Championship a few weeks later. Seeded No. 8, Dennis had beaten the young Londoner Steve Davis in the first round by a closely fought 13–11. He then produced one of the biggest upsets of form in the Championship by despatching the defending Champion, Ray Reardon, in the quarter-finals 13–8. It is now history that Dennis lost to Welshman Terry Griffiths in the 47-frame Final 24–16, but this event must rate for Dennis as one of the most 'bitter-sweet' of his snooker achievements so far.

Dennis continued the year with a full engagement diary. He competed in Canada and Bombay again and at home played in most of the main events. He represented Northern Ireland in the State Express World Cup and was a losing semi-finalist to John Virgo in the Coral UK Championship. *Pot Black* 80 included both Dennis and Terry Griffiths in the line-up: in their one meeting, Dennis not only beat the World Champion but, in doing so, scored a break of 87 – the highest in the series! Dennis was beaten twice by countryman Alex Higgins – in the quarter-finals of the Wilson's Classic and in the Final of the Tolly Cobbold at the Corn Exchange, Ipswich. He also lost twice to Ray Reardon, in the Benson and Hedges Masters and the British Gold Cup.

Seeded No. 3 for the 1980 World Championship, Dennis had no chance of reaching the Final for the second time when the young Canadian Jim Wych won their second-round match, 13–10. The greatest personal success for Dennis in 1980 was winning the Irish Professional Championship from the title-holder, Alex Higgins, with a 21–15 victory at the Ulster Hall, Belfast. Another satisfying triumph was the Pontin's 'Open' and a prize of £1500 in the inaugural Camber Sands Festival (two days earlier he had lost to Alex Higgins in the Professional contest Final).

In June 1980, a small team of British players, including Dennis, travelled to Australia, to compete in the Winfield Masters – a *Pot Black*-style TV competition. Dennis was the runner-up to John Spencer but, in typical Taylor tradition, won the prize for the highest break in the competition.

Since then Dennis has retained his Irish title – against Patsy Fagan – and, with Patsy and Alex Higgins, played for Ireland in the State Express World Cup. Always a player in demand for club exhibitions, Dennis is also a regular competitor in most of the large tournaments. His year included the Champion of Champions, the Pontin's May Festival, the Coral UK, and the Benson and Hedges Masters. In the World Championship Dennis was losing 9–11 to Kirk Stevens in the first round when he rallied to take the last four games in a row to win 13–11. However, his second-round match did not go his way as his opponent, Doug Mountjoy, progressed on his way to the Final with a 13–8 victory over the Irishman.

After a promising start in the 1981 Jameson Whiskey Trophy, having defeated Dave Martin, John Virgo and Rex Williams to reach the Final, Dennis discovered his opponent, Steve Davis, to be in devastating form. Dennis lost by 9 frames to nil! He also lost 5–4 to Doug Mountjoy in the quarter-finals of the Northern Ireland Classic but later had the satisfaction of beating Alex Higgins 16–13 to win the Irish Professional title for the third year in succession. He was the fifth seed for the 1982 World Championship, but his game against the South African Silvino Francisco provided one of the many first-round shock results when he lost by 10 frames to 7. Dennis was a semi-finalist in the 1982 Lang's Scottish Masters where he lost to Steve Davis, and a quarter-finalist in the Jameson International. He lost again to Davis in the semi-finals of the Tolly Cobbold Classic. Understandably disappointed, Dennis graciously accepted the loss of his Irish Professional title, 16–11, to Alex Higgins at the Maysfield Leisure Centre, Belfast, in March 1983. At Goffs Sales Ring, County Kildare, he lost his first round match 5–4 to Londoner Jimmy White. Despite wearing a 'giant-sized' pair of snooker spectacles, specially designed for him by Jack Karnehm, Dennis, the thirteenth seed, found that number unlucky in the 1983 World Championship, going out in the second round against the eventual champion Steve Davis by 13 frames to 11!

Later that year he was beaten 5–3 by Cliff Thorburn in the first round of the Jameson International and was a member of the Northern Ireland team which reached the semi-finals of the State Express World Team Classic. Dennis lost 9–4 to Jimmy White in the second round of the Coral UK and 5–2 to Tony Knowles in the first round of the Benson and Hedges Masters.

He won the *Pot Black* highest break prize in 1984, for the second time, with a score of 81 and was narrowly beaten, 6–5, by Terry Griffiths in the semi-finals of the Benson and Hedges Irish Masters. In a bold attempt to win the 1984 World Championship (he was a finalist in 1979) by victories over Joe Johnson, 10–1, John Parrott, 13–11, and in the quarter-finals, Doug Mountjoy, 13–8, Dennis, seeded 13, met Steve Davis again in the semi-finals and lost by 16 frames to 9. Another player who combines commentating with cueing, Dennis is now up-graded to No.10 in the World Ranking List.

Cliff Thorburn

Cliff Thorburn, from Ontario, Canada, was the 1972 North American and Canadian Professional Champion but lost both titles to Bill Werbeniuk in 1973. On his first visit to England in 1973 he competed in the World Professional Snooker Championship, defeating Dennis Taylor 9–8 in the first round and narrowly losing 15–16 to Rex Williams in the second round. He then entered the Plate Competition and lost 15–16 to John Pulman in the Final. He reached the quarter-finals of the World Open Snooker Championship in November 1973 when he was defeated 2–5.

Thorburn's début on *Pot Black* was hampered by an attack of flu and he did not play at his best until the third game. He won convincingly enough against Jack Rea but did not qualify for the semi-finals.

Thorburn did not progress beyond the first round of the 1974 World Professional Championships. However, he regained his form and confidence later in the year when he won the televised Australian Masters Tournament in Melbourne, beating John Spencer in the Final.

Back in Canada, Thorburn won another major tournament by beating Dennis Taylor of Blackburn by 8 frames to 6 in the Final. Said Taylor, 'Cliff is a very difficult player to beat on his home ground.'

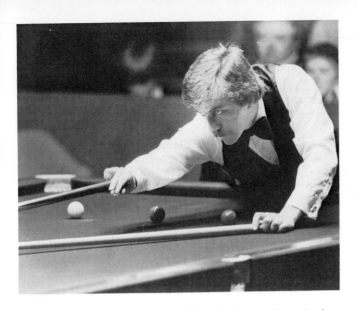

Thorburn is also well suited by the Australian playing conditions as his performance in the 1975 World Championship showed. He defeated *Pot Black* Champion Graham Miles in the second round 15–2 and lost by seven frames to Eddie Charlton in the quarter-finals.

Cliff retained the Canadian Professional title in 1976 from Bill Werbeniuk by 11–1. He lost by 14 frames to 15 against Alex Higgins in the first round of the 1976 World Championship.

Cliff made a big impression with the snooker fans at Sheffield in 1977 when, returning to England for another attempt at the World title, he disposed of Rex Williams, Eddie Charlton and Dennis Taylor to reach the Final against John Spencer. At one point the Canadian held Spencer 18 frames to 18, but then Spencer drew steadily ahead and Cliff conceded the last and final frame with the scores Spencer 25, Thorburn 21.

Cliff's quarter-final game against Eddie Charlton in the 1978 World Championship ended his chances of any further progress when he lost 13 frames to 12 after leading by 12 to 8. Later in the year Cliff won the $6000 first prize in the Open tournament at the Canadian National Exhibition Centre in Toronto by beating the young Londoner Tony Meo 17–15. An audience of around 1500 watched the exciting Final in the packed match hall where Cliff Thorburn not only won the title, but was the first Canadian to have his name inscribed on the trophy.

Cliff competed in the Holsten Lager Tournament at Slough in the winter of 1979 but went out in the second round to John Spencer. In one of the frames he sat and watched John take every ball to score a 147 maximum! 'It was an honour to be part of a piece of history' was the Canadian's verdict. On to the World Championship, where Cliff was the No. 5 seed, but lost to John Virgo in the first round 13–10. Some consolation for Cliff came in one winning frame with a break of 125.

In September 1979 Cliff won his third Canadian Open – from the world champion, Terry Griffiths – by the slenderest of margins, 17–16. He returned to England the following month as a member of the Canadian trio for the State Express World Challenge Cup. They were beaten by the England and Australia teams, but Cliff had the distinction of scoring the highest break in the tournament with 126 (against Terry Griffiths). The Canadian and the Welshman met yet again in the 1980 Benson and Hedges Masters where Griffiths, the eventual winner, beat Thorburn 5–3 in the quarter-finals.

As a former finalist in the 1977 World Championship, the odds of 14 to 1 offered against Thorburn before the start of the 1980 Championship were, perhaps, somewhat generous. They rapidly shortened, however, as the thirty-two-year-old Canadian Champion defeated, in turn, Doug Mountjoy, Jim Wych and David Taylor to reach the Final against Alex Higgins. Cliff's first World title, won by 18 frames to 16, was well earned, especially the winner's cheque for £15,000!

With the increased value and attraction of sponsored competitions, Cliff and his Canadian colleagues now find it worthwhile to be almost permanently based in the UK. In September 1980, though, Cliff did return to Canada to defend his Canadian Open title successfully against Terry Griffiths, 17–10, in the Final played in Toronto. Then he and his 'team', Bill Werbeniuk and Kirk Stevens, were the runners-up to Wales in the State Express World Cup at the New London Theatre in October. In the Benson and Hedges Masters in January 1981 Cliff lost in the semi-finals to Alex Higgins, and Terry Griffiths defeated him in the Benson and Hedges Irish Masters, Dublin, again in the semi-finals, in February. Despite three previous appearances in *Pot Black*, Cliff had never reached the Final, but in *Pot Black* 81 he did, winning his first *Pot Black* Trophy against fellow countryman Jim Wych. Back at the Crucible Theatre in Sheffield Cliff was one of the favourites for the World Championship title, but became one of Steve Davis's 'victims', losing in the semi-finals 16–10.

Cliff's form declined unexpectedly in the 1981–2 season and he failed to win any major event. He was runner-up to Jimmy White in the Scottish Masters and a semi-finalist in the Yamaha Trophy. His biggest and most upsetting defeat was again delivered by Jimmy White who knocked out the second seed in the first round of the 1982 World Championship by 10 frames to 4.

A disillusioned Canadian went home to Toronto to recuperate and reflect. Upon his return to the UK Cliff captained the winning team in the 1982 State Express World Classic and was a quarter-finalist in the Lada Classic. At Wembley Conference Centre he was back in his stride, defeating Joe Johnson, Terry Griffiths, Eddie Charlton and Ray Reardon to become the 1983 Benson and Hedges Masters Champion. His confidence suitably restored, Cliff again fought his way through to the Final of the World Championship at Sheffield. Millions of BBC TV viewers had previously watched him compile his record break of 147 in the second round during a 13–12 victory over Terry Griffiths. In a rather one-sided Final, however, Cliff could not overcome Steve Davis, losing 18–6. In Sydney Cliff won the Winfield Masters – the Australian TV series based on the *Pot Black* format – against Bill Werbeniuk, again making the highest break in the competition, but this time only 129.

After a well-earned 9–8 victory against Terry Griffiths in the semi-finals of the 1983 Jameson International Cliff once more faced Steve Davis in the Final but failed to reverse their placings at Sheffield, losing by 9 frames to 4.

Cliff continued to play consistently without clinching any first prizes. He was beaten 6–2 by Tony Knowles in the Lang's Scottish Masters semi-finals and, captaining Canada, lost to England in the semi-finals of the State Express World Team Classic. In the Hofmeister World Doubles, partnered by John Virgo, Cliff was again a losing semi-finalist but, solo, lost 5–4 to John Spencer in the first round of the Benson and Hedges Masters. He was a losing semi-finalist to Tony Knowles in the Tolly Cobbold Classic and beaten 5–2 by Dennis Taylor in the Benson and Hedges Irish Masters quarter-finals.

In the 1984 World Championship, Cliff had an easy win, 10–3, against fellow-Canadian Mario Morra in the first round, followed by a tougher match against Willie Thorne in the second, winning 13–11. Playing in the quarter-finals for the second year running, Cliff got no further, losing 13–8 to Jimmy White. Cliff is still ranked as the world's No.3.

Willie Thorne

When Willie Thorne joined the *Pot Black* team of 1976 at the age of twenty-one, he was the youngest professional yet to appear in the series. He lives in Leicester and started his playing career at the Anstey Conservative Club at the age of thirteen. By seventeen he was an amateur snooker international and, two years later, became the junior Snooker and Billiards Champion.

He has beaten, at one time or another, almost all of Britain's leading amateurs and was the losing finalist in the 1975 National Amateur Championships. He defeated the 1976 *Pot Black* Champion, John Spencer, in the Canadian Open in Toronto in September 1975 – a performance which got his professional career off to a promising start.

Willie found himself somewhat overwhelmed by the opposition in the 1976 *Pot Black* series, but enjoyed a happier time the next year, beating Dennis Taylor and Graham Miles and becoming a semi-finalist. He lost to Perrie Mans in the second semi-final and then to Cliff Thorburn in the play-off for third place.

Willie's record in the 1977 and 1978 World Championships was moderate. He was beaten in both his first-round games, by Graham Miles in 1977 and Eddie Charlton in 1978, although it is only fair to say that this last defeat was by the odd frame in twenty-five.

In November 1978 he enjoyed a first-round success against Ray Reardon in the UK Championship, winning 9–6. His next game, in the quarter-finals, was less than satisfying for Willie with a 9–1 defeat by Graham Miles.

He narrowly lost 5–4 against Dennis Taylor in the Lucania Pro-Am at Romford, although he scored a break of 116 in the seventh frame, the highest break that had been made by a professional at that particular venue. Willie achieved three similar records during a tour of Scotland including a 140 total clearance on his first visit to the table at the Queen's Club, Glasgow.

In the preliminary round of the 1979 World Championship he had an easy win over Jim Charlton, Eddie's brother, 9–3. His next opponent was John Virgo and this match between two promising professionals turned out to be a minor classic. At one stage Willie was leading 8–5 but Virgo took the next four frames to win 9–8. In the 1979 Coral UK Willie lost his third-round game against Dennis Taylor by 9 frames to 8, after beating Roy Andrewartha, 9–4, in the second. On next to the Padmore/Super Crystalate International where he went one better, defeating Graham Miles before losing to Alex Higgins in the semi-finals. His game against Miles included a break of 106. In the British Gold Cup, at Derby, he won two games in the qualifying round, against John Pulman and John Virgo, but once again was denied progress into the semi-finals by Dennis Taylor.

Canadian Bill Werbeniuk put paid to Willie's chances in the 1980 World Championship, 10–9 in the first round after Thorne had won two qualifying matches. But consolation for the Leicester player arrived soon afterwards when, at the Pontin's Festival at Prestatyn, he took the first prize in the 'Open' Tournament, defeating, among others, Steve Davis and, in the Final, the former world amateur champion Cliff Wilson. This 'knock-out' competition played over a week provided him with his first professional title in five years.

Willie is now the proud resident professional at his own snooker centre in Charles Street, Leicester. It was at this venue that Susan Foster (Tamworth) won the 1980 Guinness British Women's Championship.

For Willie himself, his performances in the top tournaments were not quite effective enough to involve him in the closing stages. In the Coral UK Championship, November 1980, he beat Jim Meadowcroft 9–1 in the first round, but lost to Alex Higgins in the second. He was beaten 9–8 in the semi-finals of the John Courage English Professional by Tony Meo, and lost to Doug Mountjoy, 10–6, in the first round of the World Championship. Willie came nearest to playing the winning role when he lost the last frame (by only one point!) against Terry Griffiths in the 9–8 Final in the Pontin's Professional at Prestatyn.

Willie had earned no 'ranking' points during the three years prior to the 1982 World Championship and, not long before that event, had fractured both legs in a go-karting accident! Nevertheless, at Sheffield he provided some of his best snooker ever with first- and second-round victories over Terry Griffiths and John Spencer. This took Willie into the quarter-finals against Alex Higgins, where he scored the highest break of the tournament – a 143 clearance – before losing by 13 frames to 10. Willie was later a welcome guest during the 1982 series of *Junior Pot Black*. He also made his third competitive appearance in *Pot Black* itself in the 1983 series.

The 1982–3 season was disappointing for Willie, who is a much better player than his recent record suggests. He has, indeed, made well over thirty 'maximums' in practice and club games! He lost 5–3 to Dean Reynolds in the first round of the 1982 Jameson International and 5–0 to Eddie Charlton in the quarter-finals of the corresponding 1983 event. Willie's most profitable performance was in the 1983 Yamaha International Masters where, although beating Ray Reardon and Eddie Charlton, he was a semi-final group loser. He reached the second round of the 1983 World Championship, where he met and lost to Alex Higgins for the second year running. There was one 'high spot' for him, though. During a tour of South Africa in company with Dennis Taylor and Eddie Charlton, Willie made a 104 break against Perrie Mans. It was the first century to be seen on South African television!

He was a quarter-finalist in the 1983 Jameson International and lost 9–7 to Tony Knowles in the Professional Players Tournament semi-finals. At the Guildhall, Preston, he was beaten 9–3 by Steve Davis in the second round of the 1983 Coral UK and by Davis again in a semi-final group for the 1984 Yamaha International.

Willie was also a semi-finalist in *Pot Black* 84 where he lost 2–0 to Terry Griffiths. He partnered David Taylor in the Hofmeister World Doubles and despite scoring a break of 139 in the quarter-finals, he and Taylor lost 5–3 to Steve Davis and Tony Meo. He won his first-round match 10–9 against John Virgo in the 1984 World Championship, losing 13–11 to Cliff Thorburn in the second. Willie's useful performances, however, have elevated him from eighteenth to twelfth position in the ranking list.

John Virgo

Born in Rochdale, Lancs, in March 1946, John Virgo won the British Boys Championship in 1962, the Junior Championship in 1965 and the Youth Championship in 1969. He has been a professional since 1976. Between 1970 and 1976 he played many times for England in the Home Internationals, winning the majority of his matches. He defeated the 1978 *Pot Black* Champion, Doug Mountjoy, in the semi-finals of the 1976 Embassy Amateur International and went on to win his first important tournament. Also in that year he partnered Paul Medati to win two worthwhile amateur pairs competitions – the Joe Coral and the Double Diamond.

Virgo has played in each World Championship since 1977. In that year he lost 13–9 to John Spencer in the first round and in 1978 was narrowly beaten by Fred Davis, 9–8, in the qualifying round. The 1979 Championship proved to be much more satisfactory. John showed his best form to date by winning his game in the preliminary round 9–0 against Maurice Parkin of Sheffield, and the qualifying round tie by 9–8 against Willie Thorne. In the first round, with the pace getting hotter, John beat Cliff Thorburn of Canada 13–10, and another Canadian, Bill Werbeniuk, 13–9 in the quarter-finals. John was now in the semi-finals of the World Championship for the first time in his career, but lost to Dennis Taylor 19–12. In the play-off for third place between the two losing semi-finalists, Eddie Charlton beat Virgo 7–3.

At the end of 1979, however, John had scored his biggest success since turning professional. At the Guild-hall, Preston, he took the first prize, a trophy and £4500, upon winning the Coral UK Championship. His opponent in the Final was the 1979 World Champion Terry Griffiths and, after a drama-packed contest during which Virgo forfeited two frames to Griffiths for arriving late at a session, the result was Virgo 14 frames, Griffiths 13. 'To say it's the biggest breakthrough in my career is an under-statement' was John's immediate reaction. He maintained his new-found form shortly afterwards, winning the Bombay International Tournament against Cliff Thorburn by 13–7 in a two-day Final.

1980 was not quite so lucky for John as far as the World Championship was concerned. He had an easy win over Jim Meadowcroft in the first round, but his tremendous effort to survive the next ended with a one-frame defeat by Eddie Charlton, 13–12. John's disappointment at losing to Charlton, coupled with 'still feeling in peak condition', resulted in a compensating victory for him within a very short time. At the 1980 Pontin's Professional Tournament at Prestatyn he won the £2000 first prize, beating the two Davises, Fred and Steve, and then Ray Reardon in the Final, 9–6. Virgo made a 96 clearance in the last, winning frame.

At the New London Theatre in October 1980, John beat Kirk Stevens, Dennis Taylor, Steve Davis and Ray Rear-don in Group A for the Champion of Champions title. In the Final both he and Doug Mountjoy missed several frame-winning chances, but Mountjoy eventually won 10–8. John competed with less success in the Coral UK, losing to Tony Meo in the second round 9–1, and finished without a win in his group for the Yamaha Organs Trophy. Seeded No. 12, John lost, yet again, to Tony Meo in the first round of the 1981 World Championship by 10 frames to 6.

At Derby, in the spring of 1982, John reached the semi-finals of the Yamaha Trophy, going out to Steve Davis, 2–0. Later, at Sheffield, the thirteenth seed found that figure to be an unlucky omen in the second round of the World Championship when, having previously beaten Mike Hallett, he failed against Ray Reardon by 13 frames to 8. During the televised championship John displayed part of his 'cabaret act' consisting of impersonations of his snooker colleagues.

John played well in the 1982 Jameson International and the Professional Players tournament, reaching the semi-finals in both events. In the Coral UK he was a quarter-finalist, losing 9–6 to Tony Meo. Losses, however, followed for John, 5–1, against Doug Mountjoy in the first round of the Benson and Hedges Masters, 5–2 against Eddie Charlton in the first round of the Lada Classic at Warrington, and 10–3 against Willie Thorne, again in the first round, in the 1983 World Championship.

John, who competed in several of the TV tournaments of the 1983–4 season, had one notable triumph – the untelevised Professional Snooker League. This inaugural event, held at different venues and similar to a soccer league, ended in April with John at the top of the table. Otherwise, he achieved only modest results – his best being in the Hofmeister World Doubles, where in partnership with Cliff Thorburn he reached the semi-finals, and a one-frame defeat, 10–9, by Willie Thorne in the first round of the 1984 World Championship.

Bill Werbeniuk

'Big Bill', a former Canadian champion, was born in Winnipeg and subsequently lived in Vancouver. He turned professional at the age of twenty-six in 1973. Throughout the seventies Werbeniuk has been a constant threat to the supremacy of his fellow-countryman Cliff Thorburn. He is well known as a powerful hitter of the ball, which is understandable when you consider that his weight fluctuates between 16 and 18 stone!

Bill has been a regular visitor to the UK for the past few years and had become a familiar 'figure' to the spectators at the World Snooker Championships in which his performance has been improving over the years. In 1974 and 1976 he did not survive beyond the second rounds, beaten on each occasion by Fred Davis. At Sheffield in April 1978 he defeated John Pulman to gain a place in the quarter-finals, only to find Ray Reardon too good for him by 13 frames to 6. This experience was, nevertheless, valuable to him and Bill entered the 1979 Championship with increased confidence. After beating Roy Andrewartha 9–2 in the qualifying round, he caused one of the major sensations of the tournament with his 13–11 victory over former World Champion John Spencer, the No. 4 seed. Bill then met John Virgo in the quarter-finals and, although losing 13–9, the Canadian had the satisfaction of scoring the highest break in the competition (142). This equalled the record of the highest break of 142 in a World Championship by Rex Williams.

Back on his home territory for the 1979 Canadian 'International' Bill was beaten 9–5 by Alex Higgins in the quarter-finals, and he also lost to Perrie Mans in the Padmore/Super Crystalate. He was a semi-finalist in the 1979 Coral UK Championship but was outclassed on this occasion by Terry Griffiths, 9–3. He failed to reach the semi-finals of the British Gold Cup Tournament or to last

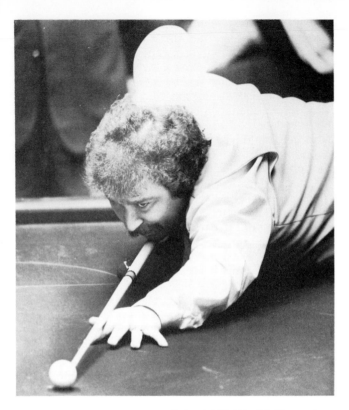

beyond the second round of the 1980 World Championship, being beaten in each instance by the same player –
Ray Reardon.

Bill has resided in England for some time now and was
appointed resident professional at promoter Mike
Watterson's new club, the Sheffield Snooker Centre, in
the summer of 1980.

Playing for Canada, along with Kirk Stevens and Cliff
Thorburn, in the State Express World Cup Bill had
individual successes in the early stages against Ray
Reardon, Doug Mountjoy, Fred Davis, John Virgo and
David Taylor. But, in the Final against Wales, he was the
loser, in turn, to each of the winning Welsh team,
Reardon, Mountjoy and Griffiths. He lost to Steve Davis,
9–3, in the second round of the Coral UK, and finished last
in Group Two of the Yamaha Organs Trophy. Bill fared
somewhat better in the 1981 World Championship where

as the No. 10 seed he reached the quarter-finals. For the second year running, though, it was Ray Reardon who put the Canadian out of the competition, with a 13 frames to 10 defeat.

'Big Bill' was beaten 5–2 by Dave Martin in the second round of the 1981 Jameson, and by 9–5 against Steve Davis in the quarter-finals of the Coral UK. He was the ninth seed for the 1982 World Championship but, despite his large daily dose of lager, the Canadian exited in the second round, 13–5, against Australian Eddie Charlton, the eighth seed.

Better fortunes, though, were on the way for Big Bill. After being a second-round loser in the Jameson International and a quarter-finalist in the Professional Players Tournament, he shared the winners' prize when the Canadian trio won the 1982 State Express World Team Classic. In the Final, Bill defeated both Steve Davis and Jimmy White. A few weeks later he was a losing quarter-finalist, with Graham Miles, in the Hofmeister World Doubles, and then began his bid for the Lada Classic title. Werbeniuk beat Alex Higgins 5–4, Doug Mountjoy 5–2 and Kirk Stevens 5–2 to reach the Final, but here he met Steve Davis again, and this time Davis – over a longer distance – won by 9 frames to 5. Bill took £10,000 as the runner-up, the biggest prize in his career, together with a further £1000 for a break of 101, the highest in the competition. He subsequently lost to Eddie Charlton in the quarter-finals of the Benson and Hedges Masters, and to Alex Higgins in the quarter-finals of the 1983 World Championship, 13–11, after beating David Taylor 13–10 in the second round. All in all, it was a good year for Big Bill, who rounded it off by finishing runner-up to Cliff Thorburn in the Australian Winfield Masters and then travelling on to Auckland, New Zealand, where he won the twin televised event, the Rothmans Masters.

Less good fortune for Bill, however, soon followed. He lost, unexpectedly, 5–3 to George Scott (Liverpool) in the qualifying rounds of the Jameson International and was a member of the Canadian team which lost to England in the semi-finals of the State Express World Doubles. Again, in the 1984 Hofmeister World Doubles, he and Eddie Charlton lost 9–1 to Steve Davis and Tony Meo in the semi-finals. Werbeniuk's way in three big tournaments was also blocked on each occasion by the same player – Terry Griffiths. Bill was beaten 5–1 by the Welshman in the first round of the 1984 Benson and Hedges Masters, 5–2 in the first round of the Benson and Hedges Irish Masters and 13–5 in the second round of the 1984 World Championship. Bill's position in the ranking list has subsequently gone down from eighth to fourteenth.

Jimmy White

Jimmy White is possibly the most exciting and promising young snooker star to join the professional firmament since Alex Higgins won the World Championship in 1972. Born in May 1962, he comes from Tooting in South London and at school (where, incidentally, one of his chums was another young professional, Tony Meo) he began to show a preference for learning snooker to more academic subjects. Eventually his headmaster gave permission for Jimmy to take afternoons off from school and practise at the local billiard hall! By the age of thirteen Jimmy had scored his first century break and at sixteen was a member of the London Team which won the 1978 English Championship. He won the British Boys Snooker Championship in 1977.

In 1979 Jimmy made further major solo efforts, winning the English Amateur Southern Championship and then, against the Northern Champion, Dave Martin, the English Amateur Championship outright. This was an event which put him into the record books as the youngest-ever English Amateur Champion, earning the title just a month before his seventeenth birthday. The young left-hander also played for the winning England team in the Home International Championship but his next triumph was again a solo effort. In November 1980 at Launceston, Tasmania, he won the World Amateur title by 11 frames to 2 against Ron Atkins of Australia. He returned home via Calcutta (where he won the Indian Championship) to find that his application to turn professional had been accepted.

Jimmy's professional début was in the Yamaha Organs Trophy at Derby, where he just failed to qualify in his group after beating John Virgo and Cliff Thorburn. As the youngest-ever competitor in the World Championship, he was also far from disgraced in his first-round match, losing by 10 frames to 8 against the eventual Champion, Steve Davis.

In September 1981 Jimmy fully justified the opening statement above with a scintillating performance in the Lang's Scottish Masters at the Kelvin Hall, Glasgow. At one stage he was 1–4 down in the Final against Cliff Thorburn (he had already beaten Ray Reardon and Steve Davis!) but then rallied to beat the Canadian by 9 frames to 4 and to take the £8000 first prize. His second major prize was also well fought for in the Northern Ireland Classic, Belfast. Jimmy's 'victims' were Cliff Thorburn and Doug Mountjoy, before he beat Steve Davis, 11–9, in the Final.

Jimmy began as the No. 21 seed in the 1982 World Championship and proceeded to beat Cliff Thorburn (yet again) 10–4 in the first round, Perrie Mans 13–6 in the second and Kirk Stevens 13–9 in the quarter-finals. His semi-final game was for many viewers the most entertaining and exciting in the Championship. This epic, albeit swift, struggle against Alex Higgins resulted in the 'Hurricane' taking the last frame, to win 16–15. Together with Steve Davis and Tony Knowles, Jimmy was a losing finalist in the 1982 State Express World Team Classic. After consistent performances in several major tournaments, however, including reaching the quarter-finals of the Benson and Hedges Masters and the Coral UK, he was the runner-up to Ray Reardon, 9–6, in the Final of the Yamaha International Masters, earning a useful £6000. Seeded tenth for the 1983 World Championship, he lost to his contemporary, the unseeded Tony Meo, 10–8, in the first round.

Jimmy started the 1983 autumn season quietly but in the Coral UK he was in the semi-finals, losing 9–4 to Steve Davis and, with Tony Knowles, he was runner-up in the Hofmeister World Doubles. After another defeat, to Eddie Charlton, in the first round of the Lada Classic, the 'Whirlwind' blew strongly in the 1984 Benson and Hedges Masters where he won the £35,000 first prize by beating Terry Griffiths 9–5 in the Final. He lost to John Spencer in the semi-finals of *Pot Black* 84 but was back in brilliant form again at the Crucible Theatre, Sheffield, for the 1984 World Championship. In the earlier rounds, during which he celebrated his twenty-second birthday, he defeated Rex Williams, Eddie Charlton, Cliff Thorburn and Kirk Stevens to reach a place in the Final. Jimmy failed by just two frames, 18–16 against Steve Davis, to become the youngest-ever winner of the World title – a record still held by Alex Higgins. Finishing the 1983–4 season as the second-highest prize-money-winning professional, Jimmy has risen from eleventh to seventh place in the world rankings.

Mark Wildman

Born in Peterborough, in January 1936, Mark (or Markham) was taught billiards and snooker by his father, himself a useful player, and later coached by the former UK Billiards Champion John Barrie. Equally proficient at

127

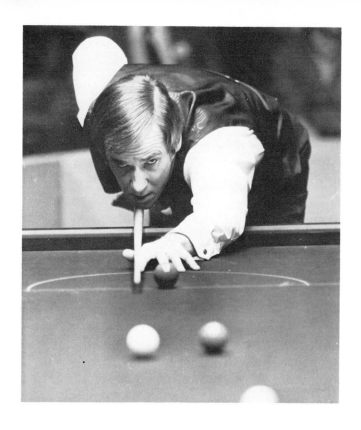

both games, Mark won the Under 16 and Under 18 Snooker Championships in 1952 and 1954, together with the corresponding billiards titles in 1953 and 1954. He was also the 1968 English Amateur Billiards Champion. Instead of choosing either game as a career, however, he entered the business world, becoming the area manager of a well-known city finance company.

As a comparative 'newcomer' to major competitions – he only turned professional in 1980 – Mark's record to date includes: Winner of the 1983 UK Billiards Championship; beating Perrie Mans 5–4 in the 1982 Professional Players Tournament; losing 5–2 to Steve Davis in the first round of the Benson and Hedges Masters; and, by a narrower margin, 10–8 to Terry Griffiths in the first round of the 1983 World Championship.

Mark competed unsuccessfully in *Pot Black* 84 – his

first time in the series – but the highlights of his 1983–4 season were winning the Strachan World Professional Billiards Championship 1045–1012 against Eddie Charlton in March 1984 at Portsmouth and beating Eddie again in the quarter-finals of the Lada Classic, 5–4, before going on to lose 5–3 to Tony Meo in the semi-finals.

Mark, who has a reputation for a keen sense of humour and a willingness to 'bet on almost anything', is the manager of the Court Snooker Centre in Peterborough where Anglia TV gave coverage to the Final of the 1983 World Billiards Championship. He is also frequently heard as an ITV snooker commentator.

Rex Williams

Until Jimmy White won the English Amateur Snooker Championship in 1979, Rex Williams had been the youngest player ever, at the age of seventeen, to win that title, which he did in 1951. He was already twice Boys Champion at Billiards and Snooker. As a very young professional, Williams quickly established himself as a player to be reckoned with, winning the World Professional Billiards Championship against Clark McConachy in New Zealand in 1968. He retained his title in 1971 when he defeated Bernard Bennett at Southampton, and again in October 1973 against Jack Karnehm. In September 1974 Rex defended his title successfully once more against Eddie Charlton at Geraldtown in Western Australia and in 1976 at the Aberdeen Chateau in Geelong, Australia, he beat Eddie Charlton for the second time, to remain World Billiards Champion.

Williams is a 'textbook' player and owes much to Joe Davis for instruction and advice. His dedication to technically correct play resulted in the achieving of the maximum break in snooker of 147 no less than four times. One of these breaks made in 1965 is recognised as a world record – an honour he shares with Joe Davis.

Rex has made several serious attempts to win the World Professional Snooker Championship and in the last few years has figured prominently in the closing stages. In 1972 he reached the semi-finals and lost to the eventual champion, Alex Higgins, by 31 frames to 30. A year later Williams was beaten by John Spencer in the quarter-finals, but in 1974 he was in the semi-finals again only to lose against the then *Pot Black* Champion, Graham Miles. Rex was beaten by Alex Higgins yet again in the 1975 quarter-finals and was unable to progress beyond the early rounds, losing to Jim Meadowcroft in 1976 in Middlesbrough, and Cliff Thorburn and Willie Thorne in 1977 and 1978 in Sheffield.

In the qualifying round of the 1978 Coral UK Snooker Championship Rex trailed 2 frames to 8 against Welsh-man Terry Griffiths before taking seven frames in suc-cession to win 9–8. An identical score, but this time against him, took him out of the competition against Graham Miles. The UK Professional Billiards Champion-ship staged at the Northern Snooker Centre, Leeds, gave Rex the opportunity to exhibit his superior skills at the 'senior' game. The title had been held by Fred Davis for twenty-eight years, but in February 1979 Fred was a losing semi-finalist. Rex became the new champion after beating John Barrie of Wisbech by 2952 points to 2116 in the Final. However, Rex, whose ambition has always been to win the World Snooker Championship, only succeeded in reaching the qualifying round in 1979, after beating David Greaves of Blackpool, before he was knocked out of the competition by Graham Miles, 9–5.

He was equally unfortunate in the 1980 Championship, suffering a 9–7 defeat in the qualifying round against the young Canadian Jim Wych. In May Rex accepted the challenge from Fred Davis for the World Billiards Cham-pionship, a title which he had held since 1968. The match, played in Leeds in the presence of ninety-four-year-old Willie Smith, World Billiards Champion in 1920, resulted in Rex losing his crown to Fred by 5978 points to 4452. He made another bid to retrieve it in October 1980 at the Brownsover Hall Hotel in Rugby. Played this time on a tournament, instead of a challenge, basis, Rex lost his quarter-final game against Mark Wildman (Peterborough) by 1476 points to 1415. He regained the United Kingdom Professional Billiards Championship, however, at the Winter Gardens, Margate, in February 1981. The competition, sponsored by Super Crystalate, attracted a dozen entries including Steve Davis, Graham Miles, John Pulman, Jack Karnehm and, of course, Fred

Davis. Having beaten Fred in the semi-finals, Rex met Jack Karnehm, the defending champion and now a BBC commentator, in the Final, winning decisively by 1592 points to 1112.

Earlier in the season Rex had also shown a vast improvement in his snooker form by beating both Doug Mountjoy and David Taylor in the Coral UK before a 9–4 defeat by Ray Reardon in the quarter-finals. He disappeared rapidly from the 1981 World Championship, winning against Sid Hood and then losing to Ray Edmonds in a qualifying group. The many facets of billiards and snooker are also displayed by Rex as the manager of a snooker and pool accessories company and a TV commentator. When he finds time to relax, Rex turns to ornithology. In 1982 Rex regained his World Billiards Championship title at the newly opened La Reserve at Sutton Coldfield, beating Mark Wildman, and was re-elected chairman of the World Professional Billiards and Snooker Association Ltd, the professional game's governing body.

Rex was beaten by Mark Wildman in the semi-finals of the 1983 UK Professional Billiards Championship, but successfully defended his World Billiards title at the Court Snooker Centre, Peterborough, against Fred Davis. Rex then decided to concentrate on his snooker playing again, but without any noticeable effect in the few tournaments he entered. He lost to Steve Davis, 10–4, in the first round of the 1983 World Championship and, a holder of the World maximum break record himself, was later in the BBC commentary box (with Jack Karnehm) when Cliff Thorburn compiled the first 147 in a World Championship.

Rex did not defend his World Billiards title in 1984 but in snooker achieved two highest breaks in the competitions he did enter. Against Tony Meo in the first round of the Lada Classic Rex made a total clearance of 143 and in the 1984 World Championship he scored 138 against Jimmy White, also in the first round. Otherwise, he made little show in the major tournaments, losing 9–4 to Cliff Wilson in the first round of the Coral UK, 5–3 to Tony Meo in the Lada Classic and 10–6 to Jimmy White in the 1984 World Championship.

MAKE SNOOKER EASY BY LOOKING AHEAD
by Rex Williams

Professional and match-winning snooker to me is not always the compiling of large breaks interspersed with many brilliant pots, but the stringing together of a whole series of shots with the accent throughout on making everything as easy as possible. Probably one of the greatest assets or secrets of any of the champions lies in their uncanny ability to find the weight or strength of any table on which they are required to play. An inch or two out can bring to a quick end what looks like a very promising situation. This, allied to the fact of being able to spot a winning opening, is the difference between a very good player and a great player – although I mustn't forget to mention that you still have to be able to pot!

Almost anyone playing snooker can point to some fantastic shot which they have brought off at some time or other – a three-cushion 'cocked hat' double, a miraculous escape from a snooker or some dazzling length-of-the-table pot – but the ones I particularly remember are those which have either salvaged a completely wrecked position or paved the way for more.

In this category Diagram 1 illustrates the point of looking ahead. Right at the commencement of the game I was confronted with the position of being able to pot the red along the top cushion. Unfortunately, the black was covered by the only other loose red. I could have elected to stun the red in and gone back down the table via the side cushion, hoping to leave an angle to be able to pot the blue into the centre pocket and crash into the triangle of reds. But even though I was pretty certain of potting the red and achieving a decent enough position on the blue to be able to carry out this manoeuvre I decided against it. Potting the blue into the centre pocket to cannon on the pink/reds is always fraught with danger, and invariably the cue-ball seems to end up near one of the two top corner pockets, with little to follow, and occasionally heartbreakingly in-off into the bargain.

My choice was to pot the red steadily along the cushion, as in Diagram 2, using running side (in this position left-hand side) on the cue-ball to try and glance

1 2

the red out of the way of the black, leaving an easy pot black into the opposite corner, with a screw into the pack to open it up, and everything, I hope, plain sailing from there on. The danger is in contacting the red too full, but played with care this is a shot that can make the opening to win a frame.

Diagram 3 is another position often facing even the lowliest of club players. It is a perfectly straightforward pot red to leave an easy black into the top corner. Most people tend to pot the red and hope to split the pack from the black, but the secret is to split the pack first with a short sharp punch shot, not too hard, disturbing the couple of outside reds, still leaving the same position on the black, but the balls now well set for the break to continue. A very easy shot – but look what a little foresight has produced!

Inevitably, however, like snooker players the world over, I do have a shot that I will always remember. The place was Cape Town, South Africa, back in 1965, and I was playing the South African champion, Manuel Francisco. This was the occasion when I equalled the world record break of 147. Diagram 4 shows the position I faced

3

4

having already cleared 14 reds and blacks, just having knocked in the final red. My nerves were definitely unsteady with the record in sight. From a comparatively simple position I had left myself dead straight on the black, needing to get right back down the table, which was deadly slow by our standards, on to the yellow. Normally this is not too difficult, but on such a slow-running table, coupled with the fact that my hands were shaking a bit, I thought my chance had gone. However, an almighty screw-shot with acute right-hand side threw the cue-ball off the side cushion exactly as I had planned, leaving absolutely perfect position to mop up the colours. Even the pros suffer with nerves, and on the last few shots the pockets seemed to close up to almost half their usual size. To this day I am still not sure how I managed this shot!

Cliff Wilson

Like Ray Reardon, his rival since the 1950s, Cliff is a native of Tredegar, South Wales. He emerged on the snooker circuit in 1952 at the age of seventeen and twice became the British Junior Under 19 Champion. He also won the Welsh Amateur Championship in 1956. Cliff soon earned the reputation of being a hard hitter of the ball with a flamboyant, exciting style; his fast, positive, accurate potting won him several amateur championships and he was in constant demand for exhibition matches. His method of play therefore pre-dated that of Alex Higgins by nearly twenty years!

Cliff beat Ray Reardon in the 1954 National Amateur Championship semi-finals, finishing runner-up to Geoff Thompson by 11 frames to 9, but unfortunately he was suffering problems with his eyesight and was forced to abandon the game for many years and turned to other business interests. In the middle 1970s he returned to the snooker table and triumphed in the Welsh Amateur Championship in 1977 and 1979 and also won the World Amateur Championship in Malta in 1978. He turned professional the following year. He lost to fellow Welsh-man, Doug Mountjoy, in the first round of the 1980 World Championship, 10–6, and by the same score in the corresponding round against David Taylor in 1981. That

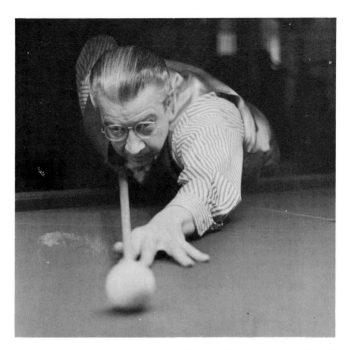

year he reached the Final of the Woodpecker Welsh Championship where he lost to none other than Ray Reardon. In the 1982 World Championship Cliff won his qualifying match against Paul Medati (Salford) confidently enough, 9–5, but facing the Australian Champion Eddie Charlton in the first round proper, the Welshman took no further part in the contest after a 10–5 defeat.

Cliff, who always appears to enjoy his game, also enjoyed a fair measure of success in his subsequent performances in some major tournaments, notably the 1982 Jameson International where he beat Doug Mountjoy and Jimmy White before losing 5–4 to Tony Knowles in the quarter-finals. In the Yamaha International he was a quarter-final group loser and, although a losing semi-finalist in the Welsh Professional Championship, he took the £500 prize for the highest break – 93. Cliff suffered a 10–2 defeat by his compatriot, Doug Mountjoy, in the first round of the 1983 World Championship.

In spite of recurring problems with his vision, Cliff battled bravely into 1984 and reached the Final of the Welsh Professional Championship, losing 9–3 to Doug

Mountjoy but beating Ray Reardon 9–4 in the semi-finals. Cliff's other best results were in getting to the second round of the Coral UK, losing on this occasion to Ray Reardon by the same score, 9–4, and to the third round of the Professional Players Tournament, where he was beaten 5–3 by Cliff Thorburn.

Jim Wych

Another young Canadian who hit the headlines during the 1980 World Championship, Jim was born in Calgary in January 1955. He is an all-round sportsman with a degree in physical education, and is more than proficient at golf, tennis, basketball and gymnastics, not to mention snooker! He won the Canadian Amateur Snooker Championship in 1979, having previously also been the 'Central and Western' and Alberta Champion. He then sacrificed the chance to represent Canada in the 1980 World Amateur Championship with the decision to take up the precarious but potentially rewarding life of a professional.

Jim nearly succeeded, at his first attempt, in winning the Canadian Professional Championship in April 1980. He beat Kirk Stevens 9–7 in the semi-finals but failed to cope with the greater experience of Cliff Thorburn in the Final, losing 9–6.

Jim was one of several Canadians to compete in the 1980 World Championship and he beat one of them, John Bear, as well as Rex Williams in the qualifying section. By winning his first-round game against John Pulman he was now running on parallel lines with his colleague Kirk Stevens. In the second round Jim was in impressive form, beating the 1979 runner-up, Dennis Taylor, 13–10, including a break of 64 in the last frame. By now there were three Canadian players amongst the eight quarter-finalists, but the luck of the draw brought together Jim Wych and the Canadian Champion, Cliff Thorburn. This was the end of Jim's road to the Final, with his senior fellow-countryman winning 13–6.

Nevertheless, it was this performance by Jim which earned him an invitation to compete in *Pot Black* 81 and which resulted in his making a special flight from Canada – missing his Christmas holiday – for the late December recordings. He made the journey worthwhile by winning

137

his games against Eddie Charlton, Alex Higgins and Ray Reardon, to gain a place in the Final. It was no disgrace to finish as runner-up to the 1980 World Champion, Cliff Thorburn. Wych, who is a left-handed player, suffered a disappointing result in the 1981 World Championship where he failed to produce his previous year's form and lost his first qualifying match to another young professional, Tony Knowles from Bolton. Jim's British engagements have not been as frequent and successful as hoped, and he once again had a disappointing attempt at the 1982 World Championship, losing 9–4 to fellow Canadian, John Bear, in the qualifying round.

Little has been heard or seen of Jim in match play during the last year or so. He did compete in the 1982

Professional Players Tournament and the Jameson International, but failed to get beyond the early stages. He was ranked No. 21 for the 1983 World Championship but his non-appearance in the qualifying rounds allowed his opponent, Mark Wildman, a walkover into the first round. However, Jim did put in an appearance again for the 1984 World Championship and qualified for the first round, beating George Ganim (Australia) 10–1, George Scott (Liverpool) 10–6 and Patsy Fagan 10–3. Unluckily, his opponent in the first round was the former World Champion Ray Reardon and he was knocked out of the championship by 10 frames to 7.

Ted Lowe

Pot Black 85 is the seventeenth series of this popular television programme and last year we introduced a new formula. The original make-up, created in 1969, featured eight players, and up to 1984 subsequent series have contained from six to twelve. Always striving to present the best for the viewer, *Pot Black* has, whenever possible, included overseas players, 'new faces' and of course its own previous champions.

With snooker now enjoying a bonanza, there are at least ten times as many professionals on the circuit than there were in 1969 – many, if not all of them, anxious to play in *Pot Black*! So, the 1984 series saw sixteen stars replace the eight-man format and the one-frame knock-out first round produced, as was to be expected, some surprises. Previous *Pot Black* Champions Steve Davis, Doug Mountjoy, Ray Reardon and Eddie Charlton were all defeated and only the three-times-Champion John Spencer made the Final, but he failed against Terry Griffiths who was playing in only his second *Pot Black*.

Incidentally, last year I also celebrated my thirtieth year as a TV commentator. It was in September 1954 when I 'filled in' for the late Raymond Glendenning to cover a TV outside broadcast from the Leicester Square Hall where I was General Manager. I had to speak very quietly – there were no sound-proof commentary boxes in those days – and I had to sit among the audience 'whispering' my commentary.

That whisper has now taken me to the other side of the

world, to Australia and New Zealand. Eddie Charlton's *Pot Black* win in 1972 played a big part in Australian television buying the series. I was invited to go to Sydney in 1976 to record their TV tournaments, based on the *Pot Black* format. They have now become an annual event. In July 1983 we also travelled on to Auckland, New Zealand, to record the first ever professional snooker series for New Zealand television. The winner was the Canadian Bill Werbeniuk.

We hope that our own new-style *Pot Black* continues to entertain you for many future series and that it opens even further venues for snooker. We also wish you good luck in 1985, whether you play or just watch!

Jack Karnehm

A senior member of the BBC TV commentary team, Jack was born in London of Czechoslovakian parentage. His commentaries and authoritative observations are drawn from a wealth of many years' practical experience in the realms of both billiards and snooker. He won the World Amateur Billiards Championship in 1969, the UK Professional Billiards Championship in 1980 and, as a snooker professional, competed in the 1974, 1977 and 1978 World Championships. He was a guest in the 1981 series of *Junior Pot Black* where, off stage, he provided the young contestants with encouragement and advice in his capacity as the National Coach for the Billiards and Snooker Control Council. Jack, who was heard and seen regularly throughout the 1984 World Championship as commentator and demonstrator, had previously lost by just 13 points to Eddie Charlton in the quarter-finals of the World Billiards Championship.

Jack's multi-involvements with the game include writing instruction books and how to play trick-shots, the manufacture of billiard tables, managing a luxurious snooker club in Windsor, and, as a former optical-instrument maker, the design of the special 'Joe 90' snooker spectacles for Dennis Taylor!

Jack Karnehm (left) and Ted Lowe.

Alan Weeks
Pot Black Compère

The 1984 series of *Pot Black* was my fifteenth. No programme I've been involved with has retained – and improved – its popularity with such regularity. Its audience comes from every section of the community; it's perhaps the one sports programme played by men which is now enjoyed equally by women. 'My wife won't miss *Pot Black*' is a comment I am continually hearing. Proof that over the past decade the programme has made its own contribution to snooker in particular, and sport in general.

My own involvement in sport has taken me through each Winter Olympic Games since 1964, the World Cup since 1962, the Olympic Games since 1960, and the Commonwealth Games since 1970. Yet it was at one of the greatest of sporting festivals that the importance of our BBC Birmingham programme was brought home.

Imagine, if you will, the mighty Olympic swimming stadium in Montreal in the summer of 1976. The building is packed with thousands of people from all corners of the earth. I am making my way to the TV Commentary position where it was to be my privilege to report on David Wilkie winning a Gold Medal in the 200-metres breast-stroke. Suddenly a whole block of spectators rises to their feet, and almost in one voice shouts: 'How's *Pot Black* going, Alan Weeks?' Every person in that block of seats gave me a wave. Where were they from? From Australia, where the programme enjoys great popularity. In Edmonton, Alberta, during the summer of 1978, I had a similar experience. This time it was New Zealanders attending the Commonwealth Games who were so appreciative.

When I think back to the old BBC Studio at Gosta Green in Birmingham where the programme started its life; when young men like Ray Reardon and John Spencer first made their mark on the way to becoming universally known personalities; how, with each succeeding year more and more people have wanted to come to see the series made,

142

and its move from Gosta Green to the newer studios in Pebble Mill. What a pleasure it was to have met so many great sportsmen, including the late Joe Davis, whose demeanour and bearing, in victory or defeat, have given the game such a marvellous image.

Yes, when I think back on these things I realise what a privilege it has been to play a small part in one of the real success stories of sport on television. I was particularly thrilled and surprised to discover that the name contained in the envelope, which I opened at the end of the 1980 *Pot Black*, of the Personality Award was my own!

Professional Snooker Since 1926

by Clive Everton

In 1923, when snooker was regarded either as a gambling game or a respite from the serious business of billiards, the Billiards Professionals Association, an organisation for markers and professionals attached to clubs rather than the big names of the day, organised a snooker tournament which was won by Tom Dennis, who owned a billiard hall in Nottingham. A year later Dennis wrote to the Billiards Association and Control Council, then the professional as well as amateur governing body, asking them to promote a professional snooker championship. A. Stanley Thorn, the secretary, replied: 'The suggestion will receive consideration at an early date but it seems a little doubtful whether snooker as a spectacular game is sufficiently successful to warrant the successful promotion of such a competition.'

There matters rested until Joe Davis and Bill Camkin, a lively Birmingham billiard trader, had a conversation about the growing popularity of Snooker which led to Davis writing to the BA & CC, drafting the conditions under which the event could take place.

The BA & CC gave their gracious consent and took 50% of the entry fees. The players were to make all their own arrangements and take the other 50% but, as it turned out, the BA & CC used that 50% to buy a trophy.

That first championship in 1926 – there were ten entries and Joe Davis netted £6. 10s. 0d. for winning it – did not lead to any dramatic lift-off. Billiards was still the main game and snooker, even the championship, was fitted in here and there. By 1931 the lack of progress was evident from the fact that there were only two entries and Davis defeated Dennis for the title in the back room of Dennis's own pub in Nottingham. The 1934 Final, in which Davis beat Tom Newman, was played over three days at Nottingham and two at Kettering.

In 1935, Conrad Stanbury, a burly Canadian, became the first overseas entrant and Davis made the first cham-

Joe Davis.

pionship century, 110. Horace Lindrum became the first Australian to enter in 1936 when, with billiards having seriously declined as a public entertainment, snooker took over as the major game, a fact underlined by the *Daily Mail* switching their long-standing sponsorship of a billiards tournament to snooker. Thurston's, the great home of the game in Leicester Square, was able to dust off its long unneeded 'House Full' notices.

The pattern of those seasons in the late 1930s was for Thurston's to stage the championship on a knock-out basis, the *Daily Mail* tournament on an all-play-all system, and week's matches, of which the most popular were Davis *v.* Lindrum. It was considered unthinkable for a really important match to last less than a week and it was hardly considered a match at all if it lasted less than three days. Professionals supplemented their incomes with week's matches in the provinces and one-night club exhibition stands.

This remained the pattern from 1946 until the closure of Leicester Square Hall – Thurston's match room under another name – in 1955. Though there were other sponsors from time to time, like the *Empire News* and the *Sporting Record*, the great tournament was that sponsored by the *News of the World*. All were contested on a round-robin handicap basis with Joe on scratch, and his brother Fred, occasionally on scratch as well, but with other handicaps of as much as 30 points per frame. There weren't enough good players to contemplate doing it any other way.

The 1946 Championship Final, a fortnight's match at the Horticultural Hall, Westminster, had brought snooker to a new peak with Joe, who then retired from championship play undefeated, and Lindrum sharing an unheard of £3000 for their trouble. Amazingly, in less than ten years professional snooker was to decline from this peak almost to the point of extinction.

Joe's retirement from championship play – when he was still the best player – devalued the Championship and though most of the finals between Fred Davis and Walter Donaldson and Fred and John Pulman brought sizeable spring crowds to Blackpool Tower Circus, one swallow did not make a season. The professionals, perhaps understandably, became preoccupied with simply making a living and there was a sad lack of both long-term planning and new faces.

The advent of television, ironically one of the great factors later in snooker's regrowth, and the closure of Leicester Square Hall, which had provided a year-round shop-window for the game, made snooker a tough market in which to make a living. Things went from bad to worse. Disillusioned, Fred retired from championship play and there were only four entries when John Pulman won it in Jersey in 1957. Snooker was occasionally seen on television, usually in the form of Joe v. A. N. Other, but nobody was under any illusion that this was regarded by the BBC or the public as much more than a convenient programme filler. The trouble was, as it was with the professional game as a whole, that all possible permutations of opponents had long since been exhausted and the results were of no significance anyway.

After seven years in limbo, the Championship was revived in 1964 on a challenge basis through the efforts of Rex Williams, who also revived the moribund professional association. Pulman made seven successful world title defences until, for the 1968–9 season, the Championship reverted to a knock-out basis with sponsorship by John Player. For different reasons, three top-quality amateurs had arrived in the professional ranks almost simultaneously in 1967: Gary Owen, twice world amateur champion, John Spencer and Ray Reardon. In Australia, Eddie Charlton had turned professional in 1963 and at

Fred Davis (above) and John Pulman.

least brought a new face to the Championship when he challenged Pulman, albeit unsuccessfully, in 1968. The introduction of colour television, and with it the first *Pot Black* series in 1969, was an invaluable stimulant in these dark days.

Ray Reardon's six World Professional Snooker titles have been won in sharply contrasting circumstances which have illustrated some of the most significant developments in the game of the last few years.

In 1970 he beat John Pulman 39–34 in a week's match at the Victoria Hall, London, after their usual tournament, held over several months in different venues, with each match promoted as a separate entity. It was an event typical of almost any year before snooker struck it big.

His next success in 1973 coincided with a radical departure from accepted methods of presenting snooker, when the whole tournament was telescoped into a Wimbledon-style fortnight with simultaneous play on eight tables. This was an innovation which encouraged much greater audience involvement and created additional psychological factors among the players. It produced an amazing comeback from Reardon, who won eleven of the last fourteen frames to beat John Spencer 23–22 in the semi-final before beating Eddie Charlton 38–32 in the Final.

The 1974 Championship was expected to be an even greater success but it turned out to be a disappointment. The echoing vastness of Belle Vue's Central and Lancaster Halls in Manchester provided an atmosphere far from ideal and there was a promotional disaster when Spencer, the local favourite, failed to survive his opening match against the South African Perrie Mans. In the same half of the draw, Charlton also lost early and, though this smoothed the way for Graham Miles, the 1974–5 *Pot Black* champion, to reach the Final, he was by that time mentally drained. Reardon beat him easily, 22–12, to retain his title.

The 1975 Championship was staged in Australia and Charlton made a great effort to win the title in front of his own people. He beat the two Canadians, Bill Werbeniuk and Cliff Thorburn, and Dennis Taylor to reach the Final, where he faced Reardon who had come through at the expense of Spencer and Alex Higgins. It was a remarkable contest. Reardon led 16–8, but Charlton won the next

Ray Reardon.

nine frames to lead 17–16. Reardon then fought back to lead 22–20, but a winning streak of eight frames in succession put the Australian 28–23 and needing only three of the last ten frames to clinch the title. Again the pendulum swung and, when Charlton missed a not too difficult brown which would have put him 30–25, Reardon's late run began to gather momentum. Eventually it reached 30–30, but Reardon made a break of 62 to win the last frame and the title.

The 1976 Championship Final, for the third time in four years, was held in Manchester, this time at Wythenshawe Forum. Experimentally, the top half of the 16-man draw – after two qualifying events at Southport and Blackpool – was staged in Middlesbrough with the bottom half at

Wythenshawe. Ray Reardon began in Middlesbrough with emphatic wins over John Dunning, Dennis Taylor and Perrie Mans, who had become the first South African ever to reach the world semi-final, by beating Graham Miles and Jim Meadowcroft. Meanwhile in Manchester Alex Higgins, wayward, unpredictable and exciting as ever, had survived three desperate finishes to reach the Final for the first time since his storybook capture of the title at his first attempt in 1972. He won the last three frames to beat Cliff Thorburn 15–14, and shaved home against John Spencer in another 15–14 finish in the quarters, before beating Charlton 15–13 in the semi-final.

It was Reardon who had to travel for the Final to a venue in which his opponent had been playing for over a week, and it did not make the atmosphere any more harmonious when it was discovered that the match table was far from perfect. Higgins led 4–2 and 10–9 but Reardon always seemed to have enough in reserve for when he really needed it and eventually, as Higgins faded, won very comfortably, 27–16.

In 1977, notwithstanding the fine matches which were contested in the later stages, the match of the tournament came in the first round when Doug Mountjoy, with an amazing final black along the side cushion, beat Alex Higgins 13–12. John Pulman, who had his best championship since he reached the Final in 1970, scored another exciting 13–12 first-round success over Fred Davis, and John Spencer, from 4–7, fought off the challenge of John Virgo, one of several hungry young professionals trying to break into the very top class, 13–9. There was another 13–12 finish in the quarter-finals when Cliff Thorburn, after a 62-minute deciding frame, beat Eddie Charlton; Dennis Taylor reached the semi-final for the second time in three years by beating Mountjoy 13–11; Pulman beat Graham Miles who, since reaching the 1974 Final, had not much distinguished himself in the Championship, 13–10, and sensationally in the result but somewhat tepidly as the match unfolded, Spencer beat Ray Reardon, champion for the previous four years, 13–6.

Down 3–7, Spencer grew stronger as Pulman faded to win their semi-final 18–16 while Thorburn, with a 111 clearance in the penultimate frame, overcame Taylor 18–16 to become the first Canadian ever to reach the Final. For much of the Final, indeed, it looked as if the title

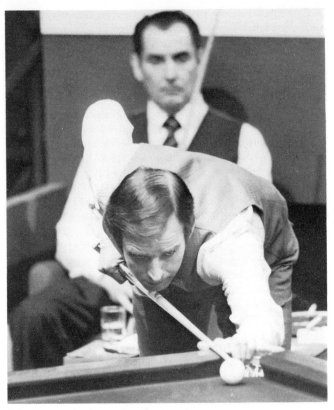

John Spencer in play against Ray Reardon.

could go overseas for the first time as Thorburn led 15–11 before Spencer levelled at 15–15 and went on to win 25–21.

Spencer, who had confounded the pundits by winning the title with a two-piece cue which he had first played with only a few weeks previously, did not survive his first match when he came to defend in 1978, for despite breaks of 118 and 138 he was beaten 13–8 by Perrie Mans, a player who had always given him trouble. Higgins, with his instinct for self-destruction leading him to throw away a commanding position, led Patsy Fagan, who had come to the fore by winning the new Super Crystalate United Kingdom Championship earlier in the season, 12–10, only to go down on the final pink 13–12; Charlton, after being within a ball of defeat at 9–12, won the last four frames to beat Willie Thorne 13–12; Reardon, after trailing Mount-joy 2–7, beat him 13–9; and Bill Werbeniuk, a 17-stone Canadian, reached the quarter-finals for the first time by beating an out-of-sorts Pulman, 13–4. In the quarter-finals, Charlton made another miraculous recovery to beat Thorburn 13–12 after trailing 8–12 and Fred Davis, to whom the crowd showed a special affection, reached the semi-final for the first time since 1974 by beating Fagan 13–10; Reardon (13–6 over Werbeniuk) and Mans (13–7 over Miles) won straightforwardly.

The semi-finals brought a moment of anxiety for Reardon as Charlton, after three of their five sessions, led him 12–9, but a 7–0 whitewash transformed the match and prefaced a Reardon victory at 18–14. Davis, despite a game last-ditch effort, succumbed to Mans 18–16, thus giving South Africa its first-ever finalist.

But the Final saw Reardon triumphantly reassert his position as the greatest player of the modern era. Mans fought hard and at times potted brilliantly but after recovering from 14–18 to 17–18 he could win only one of the last eight frames as Reardon comfortably secured his sixth world title.

With Spencer and Reardon winning the Championship, the vital ingredients of competitiveness and unpredictability were restored to the professional scene. The game, partly through improving amateur standards, became more international. Alex Higgins, winning at his first attempt in 1972, became an exciting new attraction.

The new age of sponsorship brought its benefits, not only in John Player's support of two World Championships but in Park Drive's éntry into the sport in 1971 with the promotion of a four-man tournament on a round-robin basis in eighteen different clubs with a televised Final. Park Drive turned its attention to the World Championship in 1973 and 1974, transforming it from a rambling season-long marathon in a wide variety of venues with little continuity of interest into a fortnight-long Wimbledon-style event. Other sponsors, major and minor, cottoned on to snooker's possibilities. Embassy began their association with the World Championship in 1976. Daily television coverage of the Championship was introduced in 1978.

If the seventies had been dominated by Reardon and Spencer, they ended with a new champion and the

Terry Griffiths.

prospect of a new generation of top players. Terry Griffiths, who only a few months previously had been selling insurance in his native Llanelli, won the World title at his first attempt, a feat described by Fred Davis as 'the greatest achievement the game has ever known'. His quarter-final against Alex Higgins and his semi-final against Eddie Charlton were two of the greatest matches the Championship has seen.

Consecutive centuries helped Higgins to lead 6–2 at the first interval but it was 8–8 going into the final session. It was still level at 12–12 before Griffiths compiled a superb 107 break in the decider. From the quick tempo and sharp shooting of Higgins, Griffiths had to adjust to a war of attrition with Charlton. Griffiths led 10–4, was caught at 10–10, and from then on neither man could get clean away. It took a five-hour, twenty-five-minute final session, finishing at 1.40 am, for Griffiths to secure victory at 19–17 with a climactic final clearance of 97.

Dennis Taylor, who had beaten Reardon 13–8 in the quarter-final and John Virgo 19–12 in the semi, held Griffiths to 15–15 in the Final but could win only one further frame. With a 24–16 victory Griffiths joined the select company of Joe Davis, John Spencer and Alex Higgins as the only players to win the title at their first attempt.

The 1980 Championship confirmed what 1979 had suggested: a new order of top players was emerging. Cliff Thorburn was not, as Griffiths had been, a first-attempt winner, but as a Canadian he broke new ground in becoming the first undisputed champion from overseas. He was held to 10–10 before beating Doug Mountjoy 13–10 to reach the last eight, where a 13–6 victory over his young compatriot Jim Wych, and a 16–7 semi-final defeat of David Taylor, put him into the Final against Higgins – a striking contrast in styles between the measured, calculating Canadian and the explosive, instinctive Irishman. Higgins, resisting his penchant for theatrical coups and spectacular kills in favour of playing for keeps, led 9–5 but fatally discarded this sobriety to allow Thorburn the chance to level at 9–9. The second day

154   *Cliff Thorburn.*

saw Thorburn fighting not only Higgins but the perverse resistances in himself which, throughout his career, had appeared to afflict him when he was on the brink of an important success. Twice Thorburn missed the pink which would have put him two up instead of level going into the final session; the final black from its spot, the sort he would hardly miss once a month, made the difference between two up and level with five to play; and most heart-lurchingly of all, an easy brown from its spot stayed out when two up with three to play seemed certain. To his eternal credit, Thorburn immediately put this disappointment behind him: a 119-break enabled him to regain the lead, 17–16, and another flawless frame gave him the title.

A third Davis became World champion in 1981. Joe dominated the event before the war, Fred for the decade after it, and Steve, unrelated to the mighty brothers, may well dominate it in the eighties. By no stretch of imagination was he well drawn. His first opponent, eighteen-year-old World Amateur Champion Jimmy White, responded to his chance to make a name for himself in the professional ranks with a spirited recovery which brought him from 4–8 at the start of the final session to within one frame of equality at 8–9. Without a hint of panic, Davis smoothly ran off a break of 71 to clinch the match 10–8. Alex Higgins, who had halted him at the quarter-final stage in 1980, was this time Davis's victim in the last 16. Higgins, looking jaded and publicly confessing his lack of confidence before the Championship, found inspiration hard to come by but nevertheless battled back from 2–6 to 7–9 going into the final session. When Higgins started this with a break of 47, Davis realised the importance of an immediate response. A vital answering break of 45 stopped the Irishman's momentum and helped Davis go to 10–7. A Higgins recovery thus forestalled, Davis closed out the match 13–8 without any great drama developing.

Terry Griffiths, beaten by Davis in 1980 both in the World and UK Championships, held on to 4–4 in their quarter-final but lost several long frames, including two of 57 and 52 minutes, in dropping behind 5–9. The middle session was halted two frames short to allow the match following to start on time but it nevertheless proved a delayed-action killer. Davis went on to win 13–9. Thorburn, who had won ten of the last twelve frames to beat David Taylor 13–6 in the quarter-final, tested Davis's

Steve Davis.

concentration and nerve to the utmost in the semis. Scrooge-like in his safety play, meticulous in considering and addressing each shot, Thorburn led 8–6 after a second session in which Davis lost the last four frames and at one time went over an hour without potting a ball. Remarkably, Davis's confidence remained intact. He patiently won two frames, taking 69 minutes in all, to level at 8–8, and was again level at 9–9 after the Canadian had gone in front through winning a frame which lasted a full hour. It was 12.58 am before the session ended with Davis ahead 12–10. More important, the psychological tide was now running strongly in his favour. He won the first four frames next morning to win 16–10.

In the opposite half of the draw, Doug Mountjoy, who had never previously reached a World Championship quarter-final, had meanwhile eliminated Willie Thorne 10–6, Eddie Charlton 13–7 and Dennis Taylor 13–8. His 16–10 semi-final victory over Ray Reardon included a break of 145, superseding the World Championship record of 142 jointly held by Rex Williams and Bill Werbeniuk. In the Final, however, he never fully recovered from the disastrous loss of the first six frames. Tenaciously he closed to 5–7 and 7–9, and at 8–10 overnight he was still in contention but Davis, as he had throughout the Championship, started the next session in the high gear more appropriate to a man fully played in and extended his lead to four. Again Mountjoy recovered to two behind at 12–14 to put pressure on the front runner, but Davis nervelessly made breaks of 84 and 119 in the first two frames of the final session and took the next two as well to win 18–12.

It is only a hundred miles from Birmingham to Sheffield, but it seems more like a million from Selly Park British Legion, scene of Alex Higgins's capture of the untele-vised, unsponsored World Championship at his first attempt in 1972, and the Crucible Theatre, on whose brilliantly lit stage he became the 1982 champion. Prior to the championship Higgins was not, in the inner circles of the game, thought to have a realistic chance of regaining the title, for his tournament record for the season had been the poorest of his career. However, unforeseeably Steve Davis and Terry Griffiths, who had hitherto dominated the season, both lost in the first round at Sheffield and Higgins realised that, even below his best, he had at least an even chance with everyone else. Personal ambition alone might have unbalanced him; so often, winning had not been enough for him, he had felt impelled to try and win in the grand manner. This time, he was anchored in reality by his wife Lynn and his eighteen-month-old daughter Lauren. 'Winning this will set Lynn and Lauren up for life,' he said when it became apparent that he had a real chance.

For all that, his compulsive urge to live on life's dangerous edge – stronger than any mere desire to win – had to be satisfied. He led Doug Mountjoy in the second round by two frames with three to play but, as he so often has at the Crucible, squandered winning chances before he proved his nerve in the death or glory situation for which he hungers. After that 13–12 win he again had to

Alex Higgins with his wife Lynn and daughter Lauren.

recover from two down with three to play in his semi-final against Jimmy White. A break of 72 brought him to only one behind, but it was his 69 clearance, when trailing 0–59 in the following frame, which was so aptly described by BBC summariser John Spencer as 'the break of the tournament'. The Final was delicately poised at 15–15, with five to play, but Ray Reardon, who had seemed to be inching towards his seventh title, made two errors, each of which cost him a frame, before Higgins finished the Championship with the flourish of a 135 clearance.

The seventeen-day championship had produced drama from the very outset as Davis, the defending champion, jaded from an exhausting tournament, exhibition and promotional schedule, was ousted 10–1 by Tony Knowles, who himself suffered the disappointment of a 13–11 quarter-final loss to Eddie Charlton after leading 11–6. The other pre-tournament favourite, Griffiths, also fell at the first fence, 10–6, to Willie Thorne, who went on to make a break of 143, the second highest in the history of the championship, before losing 13–10 to Higgins in the quarter-finals. Displaying potting and break-building of breathtaking speed and skill, Jimmy White became, at nineteen, the youngest-ever semi-finalist before going out so dramatically to Higgins.

The Embassy World Professional Snooker Championship 1983–4

by Clive Everton

In 1984 Steve Davis became the first Embassy World champion to be crowned three times at the Crucible Theatre, Sheffield, home of the event since 1977. He is the only such champion ever to make a successful title defence.

Davis beat Cliff Thorburn in 1983 to win for the second time in three years. There is an inbuilt drama, even a whiff of magic, in the air for a first-time winner but on this occasion Davis's superiority was so pronounced that it was left to other areas of the draw to generate lasting memories. He was extended to 13–11 by Dennis Taylor in the second round, but won all his subsequent matches by the proverbial street as he despatched Eddie Charlton, Alex Higgins and Thorburn with a session to spare in each case.

It was Davis's title all right, and the £30,000 which went with it, but in a sense it was Thorburn's championship, for the lean, unhurried, laconic Canadian was not only the hero of three monumental comeback struggles but the compiler of the championship's first-ever 147 maximum break. The 147 he made against Terry Griffiths in the second round earned him not only the £3000 highest-break prize but a special award of £10,000 for the championship's first fifteen reds, fifteen blacks and all the colours sequence.

It did not, though, guarantee him an easy victory, for Griffiths levelled the match from three down with four to play before the Canadian prevailed, 13–12. The final session of six hours, twenty-five minutes, the longest on record, finished at 3.51 am. There were more late night specials to come. From two down with three to play, Thorburn beat Kirk Stevens 13–12 in the quarter-finals, and from this precarious position he escaped again in the semis, to oust Tony Knowles 16–15.

Cliff Thorburn pots that final black.

Meanwhile Higgins had conceded his title with dignity and humour, after Davis had vanquished him 16–5 in the other semi-final. 'Steve played strong, solid Snooker. He did me like a kipper. I stuck to the honey and the vitamin pills but I still got stuffed,' he said. Knowles beat Ray Reardon and Tony Meo to reach the semi-finals for the first time and confirm his new standing as a player of authentic world class. Stevens, who was within a frame of reaching his second semi-final, and Meo, who reached the quarter-finals for the first time, also gave prominence to Snooker's rising generation.

One of the game's more senior citizens, Eddie Charlton, reached the quarter-finals for the fifth time in six years but was denied his fourth semi-final place by Davis. Bill Werbeniuk took seven frames in a row, from 6–10, to beat David Taylor 13–10 and earn his fourth world quarter-final appearance at the Crucible, and then held Higgins to 11–11 before the defending champion took the next two frames for the match.

In becoming the first Embassy World Champion ever to make a successful title defence at the Crucible Theatre, Steve Davis was only once in serious trouble. He had been extended to 13–10 by Terry Griffiths in the quarter-finals after the Welshman had led 6–3 and 9–8 but, hard as this battle was, Davis never came under the extraordinary pressure he felt in the Final when Jimmy White, having slid steadily to a 4–12 deficit at the end of the first day's play, almost snatched an incredible victory.

'I told Terry after the quarter-final that I didn't think that I could ever have a harder game but I never knew there could be pressure like this. It's the most I've ever felt,' said Davis.

The BBC viewing figures – 6.3 million at the start of the final session, rising to 12.8 million and 13.1 million for the last two fifteen-minute segments of the match – provided an index of rising tension before Davis just managed to clinch the 18–16 win which gave him the record first prize of £44,000. Such a finish was set up by the furious charge with which White had taken seven of the eight afternoon frames to trail only 11–13 going into the final session. Davis went to 15–11 but White was within one frame at 15–16 before the defending champion took two of the next three frames to secure the title for the third time.

'The Kirk Stevens match took it all out of me,' said White in explanation of his low-key performances on the first day of the Final and in reference to his marvellous semi-final against the new Canadian champion. Trailing 10–12 going into the final session, White won five straight frames in brilliant fashion but had to withstand a determined recovery from the Canadian before winning 16–14.

Curiously, the championship as a whole provided fewer close matches than usual. One first-round match which did go the distance saw Neal Foulds, a twenty-year-old Londoner, overturn Alex Higgins 10–9; another newcomer, John Parrott, a few months younger than Foulds, repeated his Lada Classic triumph over Tony Knowles, this time by a 10–7 margin. Another first-round surprise, in view of his fine season overall, was Tony Meo's 10–5 defeat by Silvino Francisco. Two of the circuit's most

Steve Davis wins the 1984 championship.

experienced warriors, Dennis Taylor and Doug Mountjoy, disposed of Parrott and Foulds respectively in the second round, which was also notable for White winning 10 of the last 12 frames to beat Eddie Charlton 13–7.

The quarter-finals saw Stevens reach his second world semi-final by crushing Ray Reardon, 13–2; a pronounced clash of styles brought together White and Cliff Thorburn with White winning 13–8; and Taylor beat Mountjoy by the same score to reach the semi-finals for the fourth time. In 1979, in fact, Taylor went on to reach the Final but this time Davis closed him out 16–9. Rex Williams took the £4000 highest break prize for the 138 he made in losing to White in the first round.

Embassy World Professional Snooker Championship **1983**

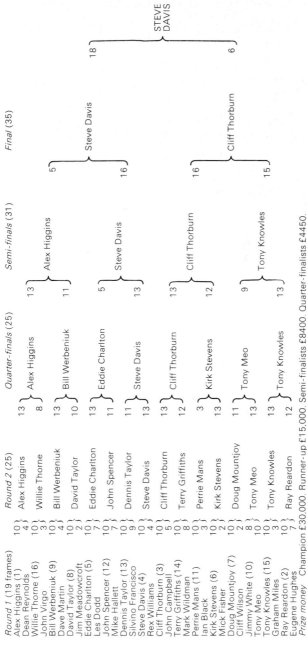

Round 1 (19 frames)		Round 2 (25)		Quarter-finals (25)		Semi-finals (31)		Final (35)			
Alex Higgins (1)	10	Alex Higgins	13	Alex Higgins	13	Alex Higgins	5	Steve Davis	18	STEVE DAVIS
Dean Reynolds	4									
Willie Thorne (16)	10	Willie Thorne	8							
John Virgo	3									
Bill Werbeniuk (9)	10	Bill Werbeniuk	13	Bill Werbeniuk	10					
Dave Martin	4									
David Taylor (8)	10	David Taylor	10							
Jim Meadowcroft	2									
Eddie Charlton (5)	10	Eddie Charlton	13	Eddie Charlton	11	Steve Davis	13			
Les Dodd	7									
John Spencer (12)	10	John Spencer	7							
Mike Hallett	7									
Dennis Taylor (13)	10	Dennis Taylor	11	Steve Davis	13					
Silvino Francisco	9									
Steve Davis (4)	10	Steve Davis	13							
Rex Williams	4									
Cliff Thorburn (3)	10	Cliff Thorburn	13	Cliff Thorburn	13	Cliff Thorburn	16	Cliff Thorburn	6	
John Campbell	5									
Terry Griffiths (14)	10	Terry Griffiths	12							
Mark Wildman	8									
Perrie Mans (11)	10	Perrie Mans	3	Kirk Stevens	12					
Ian Black	3									
Kirk Stevens (6)	10	Kirk Stevens	13							
Mick Fisher	2									
Doug Mountjoy (7)	10	Doug Mountjoy	11	Tony Meo	9	Tony Knowles	15			
Cliff Wilson	2									
Jimmy White (10)	8	Tony Meo	13							
Tony Meo	10									
Tony Knowles (15)	10	Tony Knowles	13	Tony Knowles	13					
Graham Miles	3									
Ray Reardon (2)	10	Ray Reardon	12							
Eugene Hughes	7									

Prize money Champion £30,000. Runner-up £15,000. Semi-finalists £8400. Quarter-finalists £4450. Second-round losers £2950. First-round losers £1500. Highest break £1500. Maximum break £10,000.
Figures in brackets indicate seeding.

Embassy World Professional Snooker Championship 1984

Round 1 (19 frames)

Player	Score
Steve Davis (1)	10
Warren King	3
John Spencer (16)	10
Graham Miles	3
Terry Griffiths (9)	10
Paul Mifsud	2
Bill Werbeniuk (8)	10
Fred Davis	2
Alex Higgins (5)	9
Neal Foulds	10
Doug Mountjoy (12)	10
Mike Hallett	4
Dennis Taylor (13)	10
Joe Johnson	1
Tony Knowles (4)	7
John Parrott	10
Cliff Thorburn (3)	10
Mario Morra	3
John Virgo (14)	9
Willie Thorne	10
Jimmy White (11)	10
Rex Williams	6
Eddie Charlton (6)	10
Roy Andrewartha	4
Kirk Stevens (7)	10
Eddie Sinclair	1
David Taylor (10)	10
Marcel Gauvreau	5
Tony Meo (15)	5
Silvino Francisco	10
Ray Reardon (2)	10
Jim Wych	7

Round 2 (25)

Player	Score
Steve Davis	10
John Spencer	3
Terry Griffiths	10
Bill Werbeniuk	5
Neal Foulds	9
Doug Mountjoy	10
Dennis Taylor	10
John Parrott	7
Cliff Thorburn	10
Willie Thorne	9
Jimmy White	10
Eddie Charlton	6
Kirk Stevens	10
David Taylor	5
Silvino Francisco	5
Ray Reardon	10

Quarter-finals (25)

Player	Score
Steve Davis	13
Terry Griffiths	5
Doug Mountjoy	6
Dennis Taylor	13
Cliff Thorburn	11
Jimmy White	13
Kirk Stevens	13
Ray Reardon	8

Semi-finals (31)

Player	Score
Steve Davis	16
Dennis Taylor	9
Jimmy White	16
Kirk Stevens	14

Final (35)

Player	Score
Steve Davis	18
Jimmy White	16

STEVE DAVIS

Prize money: Champion £44,000. Runner-up £22,000. Semi-finalists £12,700. Quarter-finalists £6600. Second-round losers £4350. First-round losers £2200. Highest break £4000. Maximum break £15,000.

Figures in brackets indicate seeding.

World professional snooker champions

Year	Winner	Runner-up	Score
1927–46	Joe Davis		
1947	Walter Donaldson		
1948–49	Fred Davis		
1950	Walter Donaldson		
1951–56*	Fred Davis		
1957	John Pulman		
1958	Fred Davis†		
1964–68	John Pulman		
1969	John Spencer bt	Garry Owen	46–27
1970 (April)	Ray Reardon	John Pulman	39–34
1970 (Nov.)	John Spencer	Warren Simpson	42–31
1972	Alex Higgins	John Spencer	37–32
1973	Ray Reardon	Eddie Charlton	38–32
1974	Ray Reardon	Graham Miles	22–12
1975	Ray Reardon	Eddie Charlton	31–30
1976	Ray Reardon	Alex Higgins	27–16
1977	John Spencer	Cliff Thorburn	25–21
1978	Ray Reardon	Perrie Mans	25–18
1979	Terry Griffiths	Dennis Taylor	24–16
1980	Cliff Thorburn	Alex Higgins	18–16
1981	Steve Davis	Doug Mountjoy	18–12
1982	Alex Higgins	Ray Reardon	18–15
1983	Steve Davis	Cliff Thorburn	18–6
1984	Steve Davis	Jimmy White	18–16

*In 1952 the Professional Billiard Players Association dissociated from the Billiards Association and Control Council and organised its own world championship. That year the BA & CC organised its own championship between Horace Lindrum and Clark McConachy, the only two professionals to continue to recognise their jurisdiction over professional events. Lindrum won 94–49. In 1964, the PBPA and the BA & CC reconciled their differences, giving their joint recognition of a world championship on a challenge basis. The system reverted to an open tournament basis in 1969.
†Played in Canada and not officially recognised.

1984 WORLD RANKING LIST

Until the 1982–3 season world rankings were calculated on the last three World Championships only. They now take account of other major tournaments open to all professionals and are currently based on the results of the Jameson International 1982–3, Professional Players Tournament 1982–3, Lada Classic 1984 and Embassy World Championships 1982–4. Points are awarded as follows: 5 for the winner, 4 for the runner-up, 3 for losing semi-finalists, 2 for losing quarter-finalists, and one point each for losers in the last sixteen. Results in the most recent World Championship count double.

	Points
1.Steve Davis (1)	32
2.Tony Knowles (4)	21
3.Cliff Thorburn (3)	20
4.Kirk Stevens (7)	19
5.Ray Reardon (2)	18
6.Eddie Charlton (6)	18
7.Jimmy White (11)	17
8.Terry Griffiths (9)	16
9.Alex Higgins (5)	13
10.Dennis Taylor (13)	12
11.Tony Meo (15)	12
12.Willie Thorne (18)	11
13.John Spencer (16)	10
14.Bill Werbeniuk (8)	10
15.Doug Mountjoy (12)	9
16.David Taylor (10)	8
17.Silvino Francisco (21)	8
18.John Virgo (14)	7
19.Joe Johnson (23)	6
20.John Parrott	5
21.Mark Wildman (24)	5
22.Cliff Wilson (20)	4
23.Dean Reynolds (19)	4
24.Perrie Mans (17)	4
25.Mike Hallett (29)	2
26.Dave Martin	2
27.Eugene Hughes (30)	2
28.John Campbell (32)	2
29.Murdo McLeod (27)	2
30.Neal Foulds	2
31.Rex Williams	1
32.Graham Miles (22)	1

(1983 positions in brackets.)

The Elusive 147

The maximum break in snooker is 147 – made by potting a red and the black fifteen times and then the remaining colours in the correct sequence. This total could be extended to 155. If (and it is a big 'if') a player commits a foul stroke before any reds are potted and leaves his opponent snookered, the resultant free ball potted counts as one point, and the black, potted and respotted, gives another seven points before the table is 'cleared' adding another 147 points – 155 in all. To date this total has been purely academic as no player is known to have achieved it. Thus the official world record break still stands at 147.

Although nearly fifty players claim to have made maximum breaks, the strict conditions under which they are subject to scrutiny have resulted in only two maximums being officially ratified by the Billiards and Snooker Control Council. The players were Joe Davis and Rex Williams. Murt O'Donoghue, a New Zealander, was the first to score 147 – on his own club's table at Griffiths, near Sydney, Australia, in September 1934 during a coaching session. In 1941 the late Horace Lindrum, again in Australia, made 147 during an exhibition match, and in 1948 Leo Levitt, a Canadian, scored a maximum in a practice game in Montreal. Yet another New Zealander, Clark McConachy, notched up 147 during a practice game in London in February 1952.

The first officially recognised maximum came, appropriately enough, from the cue of the 'Sultan of Snooker' himself, Joe Davis, in a game against the veteran ex-World Billiards Champion Willie Smith, at Leicester Square Hall on 22 January 1955. Even then Joe had to wait impatiently for three months before the governing body of the day, the BA & CC, finally agreed that his break could be recognised as a world record.

Ten years later, on 22 December 1965, Rex Williams, a former pupil of Joe Davis, playing against the South African amateur champion Manuel Francisco at a Cape Town hotel, also scored 147 and earned the distinction of joining Joe Davis in the record books as holder of the world record break.

John Spencer's successful 147, achieved during the Holsten Lager International at Slough in 1979, was not ratified as a record because the pockets were not deemed to be standard-size. In addition, although the competition was being recorded for television, this particular frame was played whilst the cameras were not in action; and his prize for £500 as the scorer of the highest break in the tournanient carried no bonus for being 147. Other sponsors were offering up to £10,000 for the maximum break!

It was left to another Davis – Steve, the twenty-four-year-old Londoner – to make the first-ever 147 seen on television. The date was 11 January 1982, at the Oldham Civic Centre during ITV's coverage of the Lada Classic (which, incidentally, Steve lost 9–8 to Terry Griffiths, in the Final). Steve's 147 earned him a saloon car, and the first person to congratulate him on his feat was his opponent, the man whose previous maximum had escaped the videotape machine – John Spencer!

The BBC's opportunity to transmit and record a maximum break came in the second round of the 1983 World Championship. Cliff Thorburn created a new World Championship record, scoring 147 in the fourth frame of his match against Terry Griffiths. The reward on this occasion was £10,000 (plus, later, £15,000 as the losing finalist).

Rex Williams came close to 147 in the 1984 Lada Classic, making 143 against Tony Meo, and in the Coral UK it was Tony Meo, who made a 139 against Steve Davis. It was in the 1984 Benson and Hedges Masters, however, that BBC viewers were privileged to witness another 'maximum' when, in the semi-finals, Kirk Stevens joined the exclusive 'club' of TV 147-makers in a frame against Jimmy White. This won Kirk the 'jackpot' for the maximum – £10,000 plus £1500 for a new tournament record.

It is said that records are made to be broken, but it is doubtful whether we shall ever see that academic 155 on our screens. When once asked whether he could achieve it, the late Joe Davis replied, 'It's like getting to the top of Everest and then being expected to climb up the flagpole!'

The Women's Game

The fair sex have enjoyed a game of billiards or snooker ever since the games were invented but, not unlike cricket, the sport has been, and still remains, virtually an all-male province. The British Women's Amateur and Professional Billiards and Snooker Championships (where most of the players were on the committee) were held as long ago as 1930 when the first Billiards Champion was Joyce Gardner. In 1948 the then President of the Women's Billiards Association, actress Valerie Hobson, wrote: 'I am looking forward to the time when billiards and snooker will be part of the accepted social and sporting amenities of every recreational centre. . . . Unfortunately there still seems to be some prejudice against women players.'

It is only within the last few years that women and snooker have come to be taken seriously. There are still many 'Men Only' clubs where women wishing to play find that they are 'banned' not only from practising on the club tables, but actually from the premises! However, there are now signs that matters are improving and commercial sponsors are beginning to take notice of the attraction of women's competitions and Mixed Pairs. The daily press has also caught on to the growing interest in the distaff side of the game.

The record books are now beginning to contain the names of Lesley McIlrath, 1980 World Ladies Snooker Champion, Sue Foster, 1983 World Ladies Snooker Champion, Ann Johnson, Mandy Fisher, Natalie Stelmach, the Canadian Champion, and the 1981 World Champion, Vera Selby from Newcastle, a Grade 'A' referee who was also heard commentating during the BBC transmissions from the 1982 Men's World Championship. More recently Mandy Fisher won a women's open tournament against Sue Foster at Bournemouth which included a fourteen-year-old – Angela Jones from Poole.

In 1983, in addition to the World Ladies Billiards and Snooker Association, a new company was formed – the

Lesley McIlrath.

Ladies Snooker International. The company promotes and manages several 'professionals', including Sue Foster, Lesley McIlrath (Australia), Grace Nakamura (Japan), Maryann McConnell (Canada), and the winner of the 1983 *Pot Black* Ladies Open Championship, Angela Jones.

A Mixed Doubles challenge match, sponsored by British Rail at the Cliff Pavilion, Southend, resulted in

Grace Nakamura.   *Sue Foster.*

Julie Islip and Mandy Fisher.

Tony Meo and Julie Islip beating Steve Davis and Mandy Fisher by 4 frames to 2. Mandy, from March in Cambridgeshire, has made a great effort to encourage women to take up the sport and to persuade 'chauvinist' snooker clubs to welcome women players. The day when women can compete on level terms with their professional male colleagues is, however, still a long way ahead. Meanwhile, the women have been competing in their own sponsored event – the £60,000 National Express Grand Prix. This competition has been held over several months and at various venues as a series of 'legs'. The final leg was contested at the Strathallan Hotel in Birmingham at the end of May 1984. Mandy Fisher became the overall new Ladies Champion, beating Sue Foster 4–2 in the semi-finals and Maryann McConnell 7–6 in the Final.

The Snooker Year 1982–4
by Clive Everton

Though the television viewer can enjoy a great deal of first-class Snooker without leaving his favourite armchair, he (or she) cannot thereby form any clear impression of the widely spread and various events which comprise the Snooker and Billiards circuit as a whole. Over the last few years the increase in both the number and variety of events has been dramatic, and the pattern of the circuit is by no means fixed on a year-round basis. There are, however, certain established landmarks. This short summary highlights some of the most important.

Lang's Scottish Masters

In September 1983 Steve Davis retained his title, taking the £10,000 first prize in the third year of Scotland's most prestigious event. Facing Tony Knowles in the Final – whom he barely beat in the quarter-finals the previous year – he trailed three frames to nil, but went on to win 9–6. He had a more comfortable victory, 9–4, over Alex Higgins in 1982, but in 1983 managed to set a new tournament break record, 137. BBC Scotland televised both years from Glasgow. 1981 winner: Jimmy White.

Jameson International

In October 1982 Tony Knowles won the £22,000 first prize and his first major title by beating David Taylor 9–6 in the second year of this event, held at Derby. The major surprise was the quarter-final defeat, 5–3, of Steve Davis, the 1981 winner, by Taylor. However, in 1983, Steve Davis regained the title at Newcastle with a series of victories so comfortable that his 9–4 defeat of Cliff Thorburn in the Final was actually his closest match. Davis earned £24,000, while Thorburn, who recovered from three down with four to play against Terry Griffiths in the semi-final, took £12,000 as runner-up. Television coverage was by ITV.

Professional Players Tournament

Two luxurious new Midlands snooker centres – at Aston and Sutton Coldfield – hosted this tournament in its inaugural year, 1982, financed entirely by funds accrued by the World Professional Billiards and Snooker Association, largely through television contracts. It was a rather unpromising début as it was untelevised, coming as it did in the few days between ITV's coverage of the Jameson International and BBC's coverage of the State Express. However, Ray Reardon beat Jimmy White 10–5 to take his most prestigious first prize since 1978.

In 1983 the change of venue to the Redwood Lodge Country Club and an impressive promotional campaign transformed the event. The tournament's many upsets included a 5–2 win for Mike Hallett over Steve Davis in the second round, and Joe Johnson was a surprise finalist after victories over Jimmy White, Eddie Charlton, Cliff Thorburn and Tony Meo. Tony Knowles took the £12,500 first prize by beating Johnson 9–8 in the Final, though the Yorkshireman compiled a new record break for the event – 135 – in recovering from 1–6 to 8–8. The tournament has recently been renamed the Rothmans Grand Prix.

State Express World Team Classic

In October 1982 Canada, represented by Cliff Thorburn, Bill Werbeniuk and Kirk Stevens, beat title-holders England 4–2 in front of the BBC cameras to win the title for the first time in the four-year history of the event at the Hexagon, Reading. In 1983, England fought back to regain the title with its powerful trio of Steve Davis, Tony Knowles and Tony Meo. Previous winners: Wales.

The withdrawal of State Express from all their sponsorship commitments in Britain provided the WPBSA with a chance to replan the 1984–5 season. Accordingly, it has decided to transfer the event, with a new sponsor, to a later date in the season and insert what had been the Professional Players Tournament – now renamed the Rothmans Grand Prix – into the slot, which carries nine days' TV coverage.

Coral United Kingdom Championship

Terry Griffiths ended Steve Davis's hopes of a hat-trick of UK titles at Preston Guild Hall in 1982 by beating him 9–6 in the quarter-finals, and went on to win the championship for the first time, beating Alex Higgins 16–15 to take the £11,000 first prize. Higgins came back in 1983, however, and scored his first tournament victory over Steve Davis since April 1980 to win the title for the first time. With Davis taking the first session 7–0 only one result looked possible but Higgins was level at 11–11 and went on to win 16–15. Previous winners: Patsy Fagan, Doug Mountjoy, John Virgo, Steve Davis (twice).

Hofmeister World Doubles
This event, new in November 1982, experienced some problems with its venue, Crystal Palace, but it has since transferred to the Derngate Centre, Northampton, as plush and comfortable as the Palace was cold and spartan. Steve Davis and Tony Meo won in both years: in 1982 by overwhelming Terry Griffiths and Doug Mount-joy 13–2 and in 1983 after beating Tony Knowles and Jimmy White 10–2. ITV networked both years from the quarter-finals onwards.

Lada Classic
In 1983 Steve Davis beat Bill Werbeniuk 9–5 in the Final. Werbeniuk, in the most successful tournament of his decade in snooker, took the £10,000 runner-up prize. Davis won for the second time in January 1984, beating Tony Meo 9–8 and carrying off £18,000 in prize money. Also for the second time, he survived 5–4 finishes in the quarter- and semi-finals: in 1983 against Eddie Charlton and John Spencer, and in 1984 against Terry Griffiths and John Parrott. Parrott, who established himself in his first season as a professional, beat Doug Mountjoy, Alex Higgins and Tony Knowles; Mark Wildman, at the age of forty-seven, proved another surprise semi-finalist, with wins over John Virgo, Silvino Francisco and Eddie Charlton; Rex Williams' break of 143 was the season's highest in competition. Previous winners: John Spencer, Steve Davis, Terry Griffiths.

Benson and Hedges Masters
Mammoth crowds – a record 28,297 over eight days – packed Wembley Conference Centre for the tournament in January 1983 in which Cliff Thorburn won the £16,000 first prize by beating Ray Reardon 9–7 in the Final. The event received five days' coverage by the BBC. In 1984

Jimmy White beat Terry Griffiths 9–4 to take the £35,000 first prize, but the match of the tournament was undoubtedly the semi-final in which White beat Kirk Stevens 6–4. Stevens compiled a 147 maximum, only the third ever seen on television, to earn the £10,000 jackpot and £1500 for a new tournament record. Earlier, Stevens had inflicted a 5–3 defeat on Steve Davis, one of only three reversals the World Champion suffered during the season. For the first time, BBC televised all eight days' play. Previous winners: John Spencer, Ray Reardon, Doug Mountjoy, Alex Higgins (twice), Perrie Mans, Terry Griffiths, Steve Davis.

Woodpecker Welsh Professional Championship
The Woodpecker Welsh Professional Championship, held in February, 1983, saw Ray Reardon win for the second time in four years by beating Doug Mountjoy, also the winner twice in four years, 9–1 to take the £6000 first prize in Ebbw Vale Leisure Centre. Now renamed the Strongbow Welsh Professional Championship, the competition was won in 1984 by Doug Mountjoy, who beat Cliff Wilson 9–3 to win the title for the third time, after Wilson had surprisingly eliminated Ray Reardon 9–6 in the semifinals. BBC Wales covered the event in both years.

Smithwick's Irish Professional Championship
Alex Higgins regained the title in February 1983 by beating Dennis Taylor, the defending champion, 16–11 to take the £6000 first prize at Maysfield Leisure Centre, Belfast. This event was not held in 1984.

Tolly Cobbold Classic
In 1984 Steve Davis completed a hat-trick of wins in the event by beating Tony Knowles 8–2 in the Final after scraping home 5–4 against Kirk Stevens in the semifinals. In 1983 he had beaten Terry Griffiths 7–5 to take the £5000 first prize. Anglia Television recorded the event in both years. Previous winners: Alex Higgins (twice), Graham Miles, Steve Davis.

Yamaha International Masters
Steve Davis won this event for the third time in four years in 1984, clinching the £12,000 first prize by beating the two surprise survivors to the three-man final group,

Dave Martin and John Dunning. In the previous year, Ray Reardon beat Jimmy White 9–6 in the Final. ITV networked the event. Previous winners: Alex Higgins, Steve Davis (twice).

Benson and Hedges Irish Masters
Steve Davis won this event for the second time in 1984 with a victory over Terry Griffiths, which gave him the first prize of £12,295. In 1983 he had beaten Ray Reardon 9–2. Radio Telefis Eireann televised the event from Goffs Sales Ring, Kill, in County Kildare. Previous winners: John Spencer, Doug Mountjoy, Terry Griffiths (three times).

Pontin's Festival of Snooker
In May 1983 Ray Reardon reached both Finals at Prestatyn only to be defeated 9–7 by Doug Mountjoy in the professional event and 7–3 by Terry Griffiths in the Open. There were 945 entries for the Open, in which a 70-year-old amateur, Sid Lane, made a break of 101 in his first-round match, his first match-play century since 1939. Pontin's also instituted a 'Snooker Week' at Brean Sands, in which Tony Meo beat Silvino Francisco 9–7 to win the professional event. Meo and Jimmy White won the doubles, beating John Spencer and John Virgo 4–3.

Billiards
United Kingdom Professional Championship
Mark Wildman made a break of 495 in beating World Champion Rex Williams in the semi-final, and went on to beat former World Champion Fred Davis 1500–1032 in the Final at the Victoria Snooker Centre, Southend. The event was not held in the 1983–4 season.

Ceramaform World Professional Championship
Rex Williams retained the title in 1983 by beating Fred Davis 1500–605 in a Final all the more disappointing because Anglia provided the first television coverage of the three-ball game for over thirty years. In 1984 Mark Wildman became Champion for the first time by beating Eddie Charlton by a mere 33 points, 1045–1012, in their five-hour Final at the Majestic Centre, Portsmouth. Rex Williams did not enter. This event is now known as the Strachan World Professional Billiards Championship.